Positioned to Prevail

A Woman's Guide to Achieve Resilience
One Power Move at a Time

Natasha M. Brown

Positioned to Prevail

Published by Brown & Duncan Brand Publishing Division
P.O. Box 64402
Virginia Beach, VA 23467
BandDBrand.com

For bulk requests, visit NatashaMBrown.com

Library of Congress Control Number: 2018908310

ISBN: 978-1-7324971-1-5

Printed in the United States of America

Dedication

This book is dedicated to my mom, Mary Ann Shoots. I cannot thank you enough for the times that you sacrificed, just to stand by me and for the days that you encouraged me and wanted more for me than I wanted for myself. I thank you for your prayers and for never giving up on me. I never had the opportunity to return the blessings that you gave to me, but I've always wanted to. Even though you are gone from this earth, I continue to strive to be the woman that you were to me. I hear your soft voice in my ear telling me to "never stop" and "that's my baby." I am forever grateful to you for teaching me how to be a mother, how to be selfless, and sacrifice for others; especially my children. I will continue to attempt to fill your shoes and leave the same legacy for my daughters that you left for me. I'm everything I am because you love me.

And to my daughters, Kamryn and Karrington, this book is for you. My prayer is for you to be resilient, powerful, and live a life full of purpose. Always believe in yourself, know your worth, and love yourself first. Thank you both for loving me! Greater is coming…

Acknowledgements

Special thanks to all of my friends, you know who you are. You are my cheerleaders, my supporters, and your encouragement helped me to reach this point.

To my book coach and publisher, Natasha T. Brown of B&D Brand, thank you for believing in me and taking this journey with me. I remember praying for help in the morning and finding your page in the afternoon. It was God-sent. Thank you for believing in me and for keeping me focused whenever I wanted to veer off path. I never envisioned myself to be an author, but you did. I had so many ideas, and you brought them full circle in such a short amount of time. This year, 2018, has been "all things new." I still can't believe how much we've accomplished together—whatever obstacles I threw in my own way, you saw beyond and removed them. May God bless you richly for how you have blessed me.

To every woman reading this book, I know that you have what it takes to prevail. You have what it takes to birth your vision and live in your purpose, and you have the power within you to accomplish your hearts' desires. It's time to take the leap and prevail.

Table of Contents

Introduction

Positioned to Prevail is a book for female go-getters, achievers, and destiny seekers who want to succeed mentally, socially, emotionally, and professionally. I've come to learn that there are some intentional actions that we can take as 21st century women to succeed in life, relationships, business, and social settings.

How to Apply this Book

This isn't a book that you read straight through. Instead, set time aside each week to truly meditate on and apply these power moves.

Step 1: Power Move

At the start of each week, there is a "Power Move" for you to focus on throughout the week. Review each week's Power Move on Sunday afternoon or Monday morning. Set your mind on applying this Power Move to your week's routine and interactions.

Step 2: Positioning

After you review the Power Move on Sunday/Monday, go right to the "Positioning" devotional. "Positioning" will help you determine how you're going to apply the Power Move of the week. Your goal is to position yourself to achieve each week's Power Move.

Step 3: Prevail

At the end of your business week, on either Friday or Saturday, review the "Prevail" statement and reflect on how well you implemented the Power Move for the week and positioned yourself to prevail. Each week, your goal is to prevail. In order to prevail, you have to learn and apply the lessons from each week. Most weeks, you will be prompted to journal or complete some other "Prevail" exercise. Whatever you do, DON'T SKIP THESE. Prevail pages will help you finish this journey in a more powerful position than you started.

Get ready! It's time to be *Positioned to Prevail!*

WEEK 1

Power Move:

Embrace self-discovery.

Week 1: Positioning

Experts say women (in particular) struggle with self-confidence. When you lack confidence, you shy away from new opportunities because you think you are undeserving or underqualified. You avoid risks and miss new opportunities that push you past your comfort zone. You avoid pursuing your passion because someone has already done it. Could you imagine life with no Instagram because there was already Facebook? What if I didn't write this book because there are already thousands of devotionals for women on the market? Your gift will make room for you, but it takes confidence.

I sense you asking, "How do I become more confident?" Two words: SELF-DISCOVERY! The greatest gift you can give yourself is the journey of self-discovery, and this can't be done in a crowd, my friend. This takes privacy so that you can get to know yourself. Privacy requires quiet time to reflect, so God can reveal things about you that you may not have ever known.

Self-discovery allows you to dig deeply into your soul and reveal the experiences that shaped you... good and bad. It means realizing what your beliefs are and living by them. The effects of self-discovery are increased clarity and confidence! The journey may not be easy, but it is necessary because confidence is an inside job.

Did you know there are three sides to every woman? Who she is today, who she will become, and who she dares to be. A confident woman connects with her daring side, discovers her self-doubt, and snatches her self-confidence. Confident women stand on a mountain of "No's" to get to one "Yes." You don't need affirmation or validation, because everyone's validation is not valid. When opportunity comes knocking, you will be more than prepared, and more confident, because the world woke up to see what you knew about yourself all along. Prepare to be sought after and not skipped over—you are worth it.

Week 1: Prevail

Over the next couple of days, pray, meditate, and embrace self-discovery. Begin below by writing some facts that you know about yourself. Once you finish, continue your week with a deep sense of self-awareness so that you can have "aha moments" about what you like, dislike, need, and desire.

_____

_____

_____

_____

_____

_____

_____

_____

_____

_____

_____

_____

"The most beautiful thing a woman can wear is confidence."

- Natasha M. Brown

WEEK 2

Power Move:

Be powerfully positioned.

Week 2: Positioning

It is important to understand that power is not about control at all! Power is recognizing your strength, and sharing that strength with others. You can tell who the strong women are. They are the ones you see building one another up instead of tearing each other down. Ask yourself the question, "What are my strengths and how can I use my strengths to help someone else?"

A powerful woman wants the best for everyone. She is gentle with her words, thoughts, and actions. She is humble, she knows that her job is to learn, and so she pays attention. She's careful not to depend on others to make her stronger or more powerful.

If you are her, be willing to share your strength with others so that they may have the strength to stand on their own. Allow your powerhouse personality to shine in every aspect of your life. We don't always have to have a title either. Positions and titles do not determine your power. You have always had the power my friend; you just had (or have) to find it for yourself. A powerful woman builds her own world, and she is not afraid to do so because she exemplifies strength. God gave you power when He gave you the position of a woman! Never settle for anything less than what you deserve.

Look for ways to gain new knowledge and improve yourself. A powerhouse woman reads, asks questions, and readily accepts constructive criticism because she knows there is always something and someone from which she can learn. There is nothing more powerful than a woman who is determined to rise above. Be the master of your destiny and pass it on to the next woman. A strong and powerful woman builds her own world, attracts people to it, and shares her gifts with the world.

WEEK 2

This week, position yourself to be a powerhouse. At the beginning of this week, identify your strengths and weaknesses first. Then, pay close attention to your interactions and personal successes in order to discover additional strengths to share with others.

1. IDENTIFY YOUR STRENGTHS

2. INVEST IN YOUR WEAKNESSES

Week 2: Prevail

This week, you focused on being the powerhouse that you are and becoming an even greater force in your workplace, household, and social interactions. Did you notice duties, personality traits, or weaknesses that kept you from being a true powerhouse? Write about them below.

_____

_____

_____

_____

Most women are accustomed to doing it all and it's not until we take time like this to reflect and realize that we aren't showing up as powerhouses. This is often because we are not operating in our strong places all the time. The great news is that we usually have people around us who are willing to make our burdens lighter. Today, I want you to figure out what's making you weak and who will help you be stronger.

Weakness   **Who can help?**

_____

_____

_____

_____

"You've had the power all along girlfriend."

- Natasha M. Brown

WEEK 3

Power Move:

Live on purpose and be intentional about pursuing your passion in life.

Week 3: Positioning

Have you discovered your purpose in life? What are you passionate about? If by chance you are still waiting for your passion and purpose to be revealed, I encourage you to go deeper with God. Be intentional about being close to Him. Do what you love and pray for God to lead you toward what He has for your life. Pray and ask God to give you the desires of His heart for you.

You must believe in what you do and have a passion for it because people feel and sense passion. You're not going to be able to communicate a passion for something you don't feel nor will you be able to exude purpose and power if you aren't sure who you were created to be.

I encourage you to be intentional about what you ask God for when pursuing your passion and purpose because God is very intentional about your blessing. Know this, I stopped asking God for small blessings a long time ago. I ask God for big blessings because small-minded thinking births minimal outcomes. Honey you deserve bigger and you deserve the desires of your heart! Go bigger! Go higher! Pursue your purpose in a powerful way. Embracing your authentic purpose is the guiding truth that will be a source of assurance as you try something new. It gives you courage to take risks and push past self-imposed limitations.

In order to powerfully pursue your purpose, there are four things you must do:

Pray.

Plan.

Pursue.

Persevere.

Step 1: Pray

Again, you want to pray fervently for God to lead and guide you toward your purpose if you are still in the process of discovering it. If you are living in your purpose, pray to be protected against distractions. Pray for boldness.

Prayer:

Lord, in the name of Jesus I ask that you guide me to my purpose and keep me focused this week. Remove all distractions and give me discernment to spot anything or anyone who is not a part of your purpose for my life. Give me boldness and passion to live out your purposes and plans for my life. In Jesus' name, amen.

Step 2: Plan

What are you going to focus on this week? What's one action that you can take every day to live out your purpose? Plan it out. Schedule time for it now.

Step 3: Pursue

Now that you've planned to position yourself for purpose this week, pursue and follow through!

Step 4: Persevere

Let me warn you that this week may not be easy for you. In fact, you might face more opposition than ever simply because you've made a decision to pray, plan, and pursue your purpose. When you face opposition (physically, spiritually or emotionally), know that it comes with the territory (your purpose). You must persevere!

Week 3: Prevail

Below, journal the progress and pitfalls you experienced as you focused on your purpose more intentionally.

_____

_____

_____

_____

_____

_____

_____

_____

_____

_____

_____

_____

"Purpose is your greatest asset. Pray, plan, pursue and persevere."

\- Natasha M. Brown

POSITIONED TO PREVAIL

WEEK 4

Power Move:

Always remain poised in problematic situations.

Week 4: Positioning

There will definitely come a time when someone will push your patience and test your limits, and I have certainly been there. Confession: There have been times when I did not remain poised at all. I did not like the person I became in those moments. Most importantly, I was not representing the woman who God had designed or destined me to be. I am still learning to harness self-control and think positive thoughts when negative comments are being directed towards me. Whether you are in a leadership position or not, one way to stay composed is to remember you always have an audience. If in a leadership position, your team members and other colleagues expect a certain level of integrity and intelligence from you as their leader. You are their example. Train yourself to keep in mind that you are being looked at as an example for how to behave in all situations, but especially high-pressured circumstances which calls for your resilience, resolve, and the ability to stay calm. A display of calmness commands respect and letting go of the situation simply means it's not worth the consequences. Every challenge is a learning opportunity.

Drama and conflict hinder productivity. It may be helpful to talk the situation over which can provide the opportunity to discover fresh perspectives and alternative solutions. Be careful as everyone does not have your best interest in mind. Some people enjoy seeing you "pop off" and will often encourage you to do so, and guess what, I have been this person. That Natasha was drained and has since been delivered. Thank God for deliverance!

I have learned every action doesn't deserve a reaction and every remark doesn't require a response. This growth can sometimes bring disappointment because people may constantly remind you of who you were before instead of rejoicing with you for becoming a better version of yourself. Push past the disappointment; you are positioned to prevail.

WEEK 4

This week and moving forward, listen to the soft voice affirming that you are competent and capable of handling any situation. Resolve to be solutions focused. Conflict can foster creativity; train your thoughts to have a positive perspective when you are presented with problems. Be intentional about remaining poised!

Week 4: Prevail

How'd it go this week? Did you remain poised and keep your cool? Reflect on moments when you lived up to your *Power Move...* or not! What can you do differently?

_____

_____

_____

_____

_____

_____

_____

_____

_____

_____

_____

A strong woman accepts both compliments and criticism graciously knowing that it takes both sun and rain for a flower to grow.

POSITIONED TO PREVAIL

WEEK 5

Power Move:

Be socially savvy.

Week 5: Positioning

I know we like to use social media as an avenue to put our lives on display for likes and comments, to display our talent, to showcase our children, and to simply evoke chatter. Social media is often very casual and playful. However, it is very important to represent yourself in a positive light at all times. We are all human, and we like to socialize, hence the immense popularity of social media.

When someone asks about you - *do you know...?* Guess what happens next? They go directly to Facebook, LinkedIn and GOOGLE. Companies do it also. No one has to wait for you to show up to an event or interview to find out WHO you are...they already know based on your social media activity. If your social media can't be displayed on the PowerPoint at church, then you may need to rethink what you post. Your social media profile photos should serve and complement your personal brand — not contrast it. Some women use their social media images as an outlet for expressing their alter egos, but some things are not "post" worthy.

Image management has become exponentially complex with the rise of social media and we must be careful not to get caught up in what people post because people are not always who they "post" to be! You will end up comparing yourself to a representative and not reality. Take some time to sift through your social media activity. Delete posts and people who do not positively reflect your brand. You are your brand!

Week 5: Prevail

Did you win at social media this week? Take a moment to think about the types of content that you post and the type of content that you need to post in order to become the personal brand by which you want to be known on social media.

_____

_____

_____

_____

_____

_____

_____

_____

_____

_____

"The better you feel about yourself, the less you feel the need to show off!"

- Natasha M. Brown

WEEK 6

Power Move:

Attach your attitude to your altitude.

Week 6: Positioning

Your attitude is a personal form of expression. You can choose to be happy, positive, and optimistic, or you can choose to be pessimistic and critical with a negative outlook on everything. I've learned that some people are just cantankerous—no matter what you do, they won't be happy! They find the negative in every positive situation and look for conflicts to confront. They have earned the title as conflict captain!

Not everyone thinks the way you think, knows what you know, believes what you believe, nor acts the way you would act. Remember this and you will go a long way in getting along with people. Now, I don't claim to be perfect and have been a repeat offender when it comes to needing an attitude adjustment. At some point in life, all of us have to power up and make a point to change. I don't want people to view me as having a nasty attitude. It won't be easy and hasn't been easy, but I am enjoying the transition from one version of myself to another.

Positive and powerhouse women are always winners, and their winning attitudes tend to rub off on those who associate with them. A positive attitude makes you more resilient. People are unforgiving and will brand you as "the girl with the nasty attitude" for life. Check the attitude at the door, put on some poppin' lipstick, cute shoes, adjust your crown, and represent your personal brand! A bad attitude is like a flat tire. You can't go anywhere until you change it. If there is something or a situation you don't like but have the power to change, change it. If not, change your attitude. Don't forget to smile, it's the best makeup you can wear. Your attitude is your brand and it is always on display.

Repeat and meditate on these *Attitude Adjustment Affirmations:*

•My attitude is my responsibility.

•My attitude determines my destiny.

•My attitude will have a positive impact on others.

•My attitude determines my outcome.

Week 6: Prevail

One way to remain in control of our attitudes is to identify key triggers that provoke a reaction. Reflect on your attitude this past week and identify any emotional triggers below.

I am happy when

_____

I get disappointed when

_____

I get angry when

_____

I have a bad attitude when

_____

In order to remain steady and in control of my attitude and emotions, I must

_____

"Strong, powerful, purposed and resilient women don't have attitudes, we have standards!"

— Natasha M. Brown

POSITIONED TO PREVAIL

WEEK 7

Power Move:

Don't be in such a hurry
that you miss your time
in the desert.

Week 7: Positioning

God has designed us to move in stages and every step gets us closer to our desired destiny. We see people in positions and often wonder what the person did to get to where they are. It's simple: they worked for it. Whether you think they were deserving or not, someone saw fit to elevate them. Don't spend time wondering why it was someone else's turn; start preparing for yours! Don't rush the process because you will miss the promise that God has for you.

God will shine a light on you so bright that will make you stand out when it's your turn. As you know, light produces heat. The brighter the light shines, the hotter you will become. If you can't handle the heat, then you won't be able to handle more light. That's why it's important to serve your time in the desert so you can handle the light and heat when it's your turn to shine. Focus on listening, learning, assisting, and adapting. The bible says, "Despise not the day of small beginnings!"

Continue to develop yourself in the desert, water the seeds that have been planted, and get ready to walk into your destiny. Fertilize what you have, and bloom where you are planted. You have to work your way through the desert to get to your destiny. Your only limitations are what you set up in your mind or what you allow others to place on you.

Think about the seeds you need to water this week. This is a step that will help you get closer to your desired position.

Week 7: Prevail

What seeds did you water this week? What seeds do you need to plant in order to experience a harvest moving forward? (Are you in need of anything: more education, mentoring, time, sleep?)

_____

_____

_____

_____

_____

_____

_____

_____

_____

_____

"All great achievements require time."

- Dr. Maya Angelou

WEEK 8

Power Move:

Yes. You. Can.

Week 8: Positioning

This week, your focus is on believing in YOURSELF! Are you willing to fight for yourself? Then show up for the fight, and fight for whatever "it" is for you! In life, we will encounter defeat, but we must not be defeated... get back up and try again. With God, all things are possible. – Matthew 19:26.

Protect your spirit by being selective about who you allow to speak into and over you. Never allow unqualified people to qualify you. Silence the voice of "I can't." Don't wait until everything is just right. It will never be perfect. There will always be challenges, obstacles, and less-than-perfect conditions. So what? Get started now. You will grow stronger and stronger with each step you take. Not only that, you will become more and more skilled, more and more self-confident, and more and more successful. I started writing this very book in the midst of my second divorce. I didn't spend time focusing on what people were going to say when they found out about my situation or their perception of me. I didn't worry about how I was going to explain myself. That wasn't my focus at all! My focus was on finishing the things I started years ago when I interrupted God's plan for my pleasure.

My oldest daughter had to say this particular poem every day in Pre-K3. It has stuck with me like glue.

"Can't is the worst word written or spoken.

Doing more harm than slander and lies.

On it is many a good spirit broken and with many a good purpose dies.

It springs from our lips like a timely-sent warning and laughs when we falter and fall by the way."

We can't spend time worrying; God did not create us to worry. Worrying is placing faith in the negative. If you pray and ask God to guide and guard you through the night and wake you to the morning light, then why in the world would you stay up worrying? God just may move on to the next person because you got in the way. You have to be careful about what you are saying to yourself about yourself. It does not matter what people are saying. What matters is what you are saying to yourself. Your faith has to be positive! Say this out loud, "YES I CAN AND I WILL NOT WORRY!"

This week, be aware of self-doubt. Whenever you begin to doubt yourself, simply stop and repeat, "I can do all things through Christ who strengthens me."

Week 8: Prevail

So a few days have passed, and this week should have been all about confidence. How did you do? Journal your successes and the moments when you felt defeated (if any) and how you'll fight that in the future. At the end, write YES I CAN.

_____

_____

_____

_____

_____

_____

_____

_____

_____

"Challenges make you discover things about yourself that you never really knew."

- Cicely Tyson

WEEK 9

Power Move:

Rely on your resilience.

Week 9: Positioning

When I lost my mom in 2001, my entire world shattered. I felt an indescribable pain that I can't begin to put into words. She was my everything! From that day forward, I knew my every move had to be in her honor. Giving up was not an option because she didn't give up on me. I vowed to God, my mom, and myself that I wouldn't allow anything to break me down to the point where I couldn't go on or see my way. It wasn't until a few years ago that my pastor challenged the congregation to find one word to live out for that year. I started to research other words for "strong," "not easily broken," and "not giving up," and the word "resilient" popped up. I read so many articles and examples of this word and God told me that moment, "That's you!"

Resilience is the process of adapting well in the face of adversity, trauma, tragedy, threats, or significant sources of stress — such as family and relationship problems, serious health problems, or workplace and financial stressors. It means "bouncing back" from difficult experiences. You will encounter some situations that will rock your world; whether it be a break-up, demotion, termination, rejection, or death. As Dr. Craig Oliver, Pastor of Elizabeth Baptist Church, would say, "Stop marinating in your misery and saturating in your sorrow." Learn to speak to your mountain; especially when you have been rejected. Learn to find beauty in your bruises because sometimes when things are falling apart, they may be actually falling into place! If you stretch a rubber band to its maximum width, it usually springs back because it's designed to be stretched. You will be stretched, but like a rubber band, you will bounce back. If we can avoid becoming rigid in our thinking and become more flexible with our natural elasticity, we can spring up from life's challenges.

WEEK 9

We will be faced with hard times, but these times are often blessings in disguise. No matter how much it hurts, hold your head up and keep going. Sometimes the hardest lessons to learn are the ones your spirit needs the most.

Strong women aren't simply born. We are forged through the challenges of life. With each challenge, we grow mentally and emotionally. We move forward with our heads held high and a strength that cannot be denied. A woman who's been through the storm and survived is a warrior. My scars remind me that I did indeed survive my deepest wounds. That in itself is an accomplishment. They bring to mind something else, too. They remind me that the damage life has inflicted on me has, in many places, left me stronger and more resilient. What hurt me in the past has actually made me better equipped to face the present because greater is coming…

Week 9: Prevail

In what obstacles did you prevail this week? In what ways did you grow stronger this week? Write about it below.

_____

_____

_____

_____

_____

_____

_____

_____

_____

_____

_____

"I Am Resilient!"

- Natasha M. Brown

POSITIONED TO PREVAIL

WEEK 10

Power Move:

Be a bridge building boss lady.

Week 10: Positioning

One of my main reasons for pursuing this journey was to help women learn to have positive relationships with other women by building bridges as opposed to barriers. I'm sure we have all had negative experiences connecting with other women, but please don't allow those experiences to write off building female relationships. In fact, creating a strong network of women is critical for your career and your life as we all can use a support system. Take the time to get to know others who share common interests with you and also people who are different. You never know who will be a vessel to pour essential ingredients into your life. One of my greatest joys in life is seeing women encourage, support, and empower each other. Lord, we need more of it. So I empower and encourage you to surround yourself with women with whom you can grow.

God intentionally created us uniquely. He could have made us all exactly the same. He had the power to do that. Instead, He chose to create us each by name and with great thought (Psalm 139:13). He even delights over those He created (Zephaniah 3:17). He puts us all together to learn and grow from one another—diversity and difference is one of God's gifts to us.

There is nothing like a powerhouse team of women. Having each other's backs makes us more powerful and unstoppable. When we soar together, incredible things can happen. Be a good woman, trying to be a better woman, while inspiring another woman to be her best self. Some women fail to realize that helping another woman win, cheering her on, praying for her, and sharing resources doesn't take blessings away. In fact, God adds to you and it's essentially a blessing to be a blessing. This level of thinking positions you to prevail.

This week, identify three people with whom you will establish or strengthen relationships, and make sure they are people who share different interests than you.

Week 10: Prevail

Did you connect with three people who are different than you this week? If so, how did you break the ice to become a bridge builder?

_____

_____

_____

_____

_____

_____

_____

_____

_____

_____

_____

_____

"Boss ladies build bridges and break down barriers!"

- Natasha M. Brown

WEEK 11

Power Move:

"Lord, deliver me from being a people pleaser!"

Week 11: Positioning

You will lose your power, passion, and freedom by trying to please or impress people other than God and yourself! As long as you're trying to please other people and live up to their expectations, you will not be pleasing yourself. Be happy with yourself! Sometimes, you may be too much for some people and that's fine! Sometimes your light might shine too brightly, but don't dim it! Some people may try to make you think you're not enough; hence the reason why you should surround yourself with women who push you to be a better version of yourself! If not, you will find yourself constantly seeking the approval and acceptance of others.

If there are people who simply cannot accept your limits and boundaries, then you might want to rethink these relationships. Some relationships work for a reason, but the reason isn't always healthy. People pleasing pleases everyone but the pleaser, and the pleaser will end up purposeless! Don't be afraid of losing people. Be afraid of losing yourself by trying to please people!

Week 11: Prevail

Journal... and then reflect on the type of people (including their character traits) that would help you prevail.

_____

_____

_____

_____

_____

_____

_____

_____

_____

_____

_____

_____

"The woman who does not require validation from anyone is powerful, resilient, and positioned to prevail!"

— Natasha M. Brown

WEEK 12

Power Move:

Value the vision.

Week 12: Positioning

In order to understand where we want ourselves to be in life, we must have a clear vision for our lives. A vision is an appeal to yourself to be something more. It gives you purpose and makes your life more meaningful.

It's so important to have vision and purpose because it guides us, helps us to make decisions, and ultimately creates our lifestyles. It's vital for powerful and resilient women to surround ourselves with visionaries. Just like vision chooses our direction in life, it also chooses our friends and the company we keep. People are attracted and spend time with people who have vision and who are disciplined in their vision.

It was important for me not to reveal my vision for writing this book to just anyone, because I had doubts myself. For once in my life, I didn't seek validation from anyone. I went on this journey with the ONE I knew who could help me see the vision through. I prayed for God to send me someone who could use their power, influence, and ability to help me and He did just that. I am known to be a risk taker and I am not afraid to pursue goals I am passionate about, but God gave me the vision first. I *used* to be quick to expose my vision and share my excitement with others only to be disappointed when they extinguished my fire.

As I grew wiser, it was clear "they" couldn't connect with or understand the vision I had because God didn't reveal it to them. I learned an important lesson while trying to seek approval and input from others: don't give critics the opportunity to criticize. Don't allow people to attack your virtue and value, because when you do, your vision will become distorted. When God reveals His vision for you, that vision is vulnerable. Some people will only commit to your vision if they fit into your vision. The last thing you should do is try to get others to validate your vision. Validation is for parking anyway.

WEEK 12

My daughter Kamryn shared her mantra with me on vision. She advises, "Don't downgrade your dreams to match your reality, upgrade your beliefs to match your vision. Never settle for mediocrity. Never let good enough, be good enough!" My advice to women is to never allow a blind person to proofread your vision; they can't see what God showed you.

Week 12: Prevail

Close your eyes, meditate on this: God can do exceedingly, abundantly above all that you can think, ask, or imagine. Then, allow your mind to get a glimpse of the places you'll go, how you will live, and the ways you'll impact the world. Envision a day in your ideal life. After you have a very clear vision, open your eyes, and reflect on what you envisioned below.

_____

_____

_____

_____

_____

_____

_____

_____

Remember

Now to him who is able to do immeasurably more than all we ask or imagine, according to his power that is at work within us.

Ephesians 3:20 (NIV)

"If you don't have a vision, you're going to be stuck in what you know and the only thing you know is what you've already seen."

- Iyanla Vanzant

POSITIONED TO PREVAIL

WEEK 13

Power Move:

Always believe in yourself and never allow self-doubt to exist.

Week 13: Positioning

Refuse to be confined based on how people define you, and stop allowing people to put labels on you! Start building up your emotional immune system by releasing any past negative emotions like fear, anger, disappointment, sadness, and guilt. Stop allowing unqualified people to judge you and speak over you. Your mind is your biggest asset so don't shape your mind based on the opinions of others. Girl, get your mind right! **Know what YOU believe about yourself.** Do not paralyze your purpose based on someone's perception of you! If you know who you are then you know who you're not!

Michelle Obama said it best, "One of the lessons that I grew up with was to always stay true to yourself and never let what somebody else says distract you from your goals. And so when I hear about negative and false attacks, I really don't invest any energy in them, because I know who I am."

People are always quick to judge. Let them judge you, let them misunderstand you, let them gossip; their opinions are not your problem. Don't you dare doubt yourself! If you don't have a huge amount of belief in yourself, then there is no way you can expect anyone else to believe in you! Be the woman who stops walking in the middle, because you are NO LONGER afraid to take a side. Refuse to leave the key to your happiness in someone else's hands. As women, we have enough in life against us already, so don't be against yourself.

Ask now: Jesus rid me of mind manipulators!

Negativity is contagious and infectious, so protect your mind! Be who you are and know that you won't be everyone's cup of tea. Define yourself for yourself and be true to that person. Then, you'll truly prevail. People will try to underestimate you, and as you climb higher, they will get tired of trying.

Week 13: Prevail

What do you believe about YOURSELF? Below journal your personal "I AM" affirmations

_____

_____

_____

_____

_____

_____

_____

_____

_____

_____

_____

"The important thing is to realize that no matter what people's opinions may be, they're only just that—people's opinions. You have to believe in your heart what you know to be true about yourself and let that be that."

- Mary J. Blige

WEEK 14:

Power Move:

Invest in yourself and become a subject matter expert.

Week 14: Positioning

Life is about growth! Developing and pouring into yourself are worth the investments; these efforts come with minimum risk and a guaranteed return. We must continue to move forward toward growth and choose to grow again and again. Your future self will thank you. Whatever you don't feed will eventually die. Professionals know their trades, and they know them well. Work hard and be great at what you do. Become an expert in the skills necessary to do your job. Always keep your knowledge up-to-date, and perform every task to the absolute best of your abilities. You did not come this far only to come this far. Walk in your purpose and allow your light to shine bright. You will cause opportunities to pursue you.

For knowledge, read; for wisdom, observe! Leaders read because knowledge is power! I was once told, "The world is full of knowledge. Go get you some." People may not like you, but they will not be able to deny that you're smart and you know what you are talking about! In order to become a subject matter expert, you have to be knowledgeable. Through a combination of education and experience, you have acquired knowledge; wisdom comes when you apply that knowledge. You know what it takes to do a certain job but it's important not to get comfortable in your role. Continue to invest in yourself by attending seminars, obtaining certifications, seeking higher education, and reading.

Those activities will be the best investments you will ever make because they will not only improve your life, but will improve the lives of others around you. Invest in your life work, your purpose, your relationships... invest in your brand... YOU!

Week 14: Prevail

With so many years of life under your belt, you have surely become a master at something. Below, reflect and journal about some key moments in your life that serve as turning points that shifted your thinking or changed the trajectory of your life.

_____

_____

_____

_____

_____

_____

_____

_____

_____

_____

_____

"Dreams are lovely. But they are just dreams. Fleeting, ephemeral, pretty. But dreams do not come true just because you dream them. It's hard work that makes things happen. It's hard work that creates change."

- Shonda Rhimes

WEEK 15

Power Move:

Stop allowing people to
waste your time!

Week 15: Positioning

You can get more money, but you cannot get more time. Furthermore, spending valuable time on invaluable things and people is not logical. It is OK to be selfish with your time and learn to say, "No, not now, not today!"

"No" is a complete sentence… you don't have to lie, make excuses, or over explain yourself, just simply decline. Love yourself, take care of yourself, be kind to yourself, and make yourself a priority.

Oftentimes, we spend too much time on things that don't count and too little time on things that should count. Time is such a valuable resource that you can actually control. Learn to budget your time like you budget your money and connect your time to your purpose.

Don't allow people to rob you of your time; it's not your job to be everything to everyone, otherwise people will steal your time when it's most inconvenient (for you). Consider setting expectations so people will know your time is valuable. Your behavior will train them to respect your time. Reclaim your time; it's your treasure and it's a portion of your life you will never get back.

Always ask yourself, "Is the way I'm spending my time today moving me closer to my tomorrow?" If you can learn to manage time, you can learn to manage anything.

Week 15: Prevail

Think about how you spent your time this week. Did you maximize every moment or waste any of this precious, invaluable resource? Here's your challenge: think about what activities, thoughts, and people are time wasters and need to be cut from your life.

_____

_____

_____

_____

_____

_____

_____

_____

_____

_____

"Queens don't use their time chasing things that don't position them to prevail. That will make your crown fall off."

- Natasha M. Brown

WEEK 16

Power Move:

Know your role, and be great at it!

Week 16: Positioning

If I didn't learn anything else when I was pursuing my Master of Social Work degree, I learned that as a general practitioner, I needed to know my role. I have carried this simple, yet powerful statement, "Know your role," with me through life and it has definitely helped to shape the woman I am today. The moral of this power move is simple; no matter what role you play, play it well. Whether you are the vice president, manager, secretary, server, or housekeeper, know your role! Once you understand your role, you will find that your role is tied directly to your personal success. Your role can command greater respect than your title. It's not about the title, it's about the role you play and if you play it well.

Here's another side to knowing your role; use your instincts to grow your gift. We have to do more than what our role requires us to do. Take a look at your job description... I bet somewhere at the bottom you will see the words, "...and other duties as assigned." This means there will come a time when you will be required to do more than the expected duties outlined in your job description. Some people will only do what you ask them to do and nothing more. They won't even ask if there is anything else needed or they will see you working your fingers to the bone and won't offer a helping hand. Their thought process is that *it's not my job,* or that you should ask them to help.

I was sitting at Two Urban Licks, a popular upscale restaurant in Atlanta. I kept hearing, "Hand please!" So the next time I heard it, I paid close attention (I am always observing my surroundings). Whoever had "free hands" would come over, look at the order, and take it to the table. You didn't hear anyone saying, "That's not my table!" I was in awe. What if we all could just say "hands please" and people would just show up to help. Oh my God! We have to always be willing to do more than what our roles call for us to do, and we shouldn't wait for someone to tell us everything to do. That's why employers list "self-starter, motivated, works independently, leader" as job qualifications. We have to volunteer for more, which shows your work ethic and makes you an asset, and not a liability, to an organization. You have to use your instincts and critical thinking skills in order to prevail.

Feed your brain daily and commit to learning something new every day. Consider the knowledge you have as a gift. God didn't bless us with gifts to keep to ourselves. Gifts are meant to be shared no matter how you package them. Focus on things you have been equipped to do and commit to finding opportunities to master your role.

This week, your challenge is to master YOUR lane. If you don't know what you have, you can mess around and lose it.

Week 16: Prevail

Below identify what you're good at, great at, and then circle the items from each list that you know you're purposed to do. If you have epiphanies about your personal purpose lane as you're completing this exercise, write them in column three.

Good	Great	Purposed

"You can only become truly accomplished at something you love. Don't make money your goal. Instead, pursue the things you love doing, and then do them so well that people can't take their eyes off you."

- Dr. Maya Angelou

POSITIONED TO PREVAIL

WEEK 17

Power Move:

Be careful not to use your title to taint the environment.

Week 17: Positioning

"Be careful not to use your title to taint the environment." This is a power move indeed, and you can probably imagine how many people use their titles as a way to marginalize others. This happens so often and not just in the workplace. So many people are title driven and tend to use their titles to taunt the people around them. Being title driven can ultimately taint the environment, and the same people who gave you that title can also take it away. Be careful; you can single-handedly halt your movement to the next level because of how you handle your title on the current level.

When God elevates you, count it as a blessing and find the right opportunities to hold the very ladder that someone held for you so the next person can climb. We have to lift as we climb. Don't forget about those who may not ask for help, yet need it. Whose hand are you going to reach for? God didn't promote you based on your tenure, but because you passed the test. How you handle your test will determine your tenure. The people who stick by you through your worst times are the ones who deserve to be with you through the best times.

Week 17: Prevail

How can you use your current title and position to help someone else rise?

_____

_____

_____

_____

_____

_____

_____

_____

_____

_____

_____

_____

"No matter what accomplishments you make, somebody helped you."

- **Althea Gibson**

WEEK 18

Power Move:

Articulate women are attractive, approachable, and have an amazing attitude!

Week 18: Positioning

Articulate women are attractive, approachable, and have an amazing attitude! The best, most-direct way to convey your intelligence, expertise, professionalism, and personality to other people is by talking to them. In order to be articulate, you must be confident in your approach. Think before you speak. Think clearly about what you want to say before you say it so that you don't ramble and stumble over your words as your thoughts come. Be a confident communicator! Clear, concise, and responsive communication is crucial for success.

Whether verbal or written, professionals communicate thoroughly and accurately. Your communication style tells a lot about who you are and how you work! Being approachable is a great gift. Approachability is about being accessible, having appropriate body language, and using the right verbal communication and listening skills.

Smiling is one of the most powerful tools in your arsenal to help you become more approachable! Work on being magnetizing and charming. The secret to being the most sought after, likable person in the room is to smile and present yourself well. You are responsible for the energy you bring into the room.

Week 18: Prevail

Are you articulate, attractive and approachable according to your own standards? Do you consider yourself to have a positive attitude? Remember, a good communicator listens; responds appropriately (considering the audience and circumstances); speaks clearly and concisely; and is not combative. In addition, good communicators have timely communications. Does this sound like you? If not, brainstorm on how you'll become a better you in this area.

_____

_____

_____

_____

_____

_____

_____

_____

_____

_____

"Attitude is everything!"

- Natasha M. Brown

WEEK 19

Power Move:

Elevation requires elimination.

Week 19: Positioning

Elevation requires elimination. Time and time again, I have heard people say, "Everyone does not deserve a front row seat in your life." Often in life, it will be important to reevaluate people and things around us that may not be beneficial for the future. Life is full of distractions. Take some time to evaluate the people who are causing distractions, who are drama filled, and are threatening your destiny.

Purge your contacts the same way you purge your closet. Some people never change, so stop expecting them to… people have expiration dates! Pray daily for less drama and more deliverance because it takes courage to let people go, and you have the right to do so. Don't be bitter about eliminating people and stuff, because better is before you. God will remove who you don't need and give you who you do need. If you needed them, God would not have removed them in the first place.

Friendships are not about who has known you the longest, but more about who walked into your life and proved to you that they are there cheering for you. Don't mistakenly hold on to people as a sign of strength. It takes more strength to let go! When you walk with God, you will have to leave some people behind. God placed them in your life for a season. Girlfriend, dedication to your destiny requires separation. The closer you get to where God wants you to be, you will have to separate yourself from the crowd. Crowds cloud your thought process and will cause you to miss your calling.

When you close the door on those relationships, put some tape on it that reads: THE DOOR IS CLOSED!

Week 19: Prevail

When was the last time that you purged? For as long as I can remember, I have cleaned out my closets for spring and winter, and I make room for the new seasons. A few years ago, I realized that it's just as important to evaluate the people and priorities in my life each season. This week, I challenge you to create a purge list. Seriously consider everyone in your inner circle, those who you spend your time with, and the top priorities in your life. If you find that everyone and everything in your life is as it should be, kudos!

_____

_____

_____

_____

_____

_____

_____

_____

"*You can't elevate with an entourage!*"

- Natasha M. Brown

WEEK 20

Power Move:

Be a woman other women can trust.

Week 20: Positioning

Being trustworthy is one of the greatest gifts you can give to a friend. Trust is a valuable trait that people always show through their lives and actions. I was once told that "to be trusted is a greater compliment than being loved." Trustworthy women have a loyal tribe of other trustworthy women behind them, not backstabbers. Trust is a fundamental cornerstone of successful relationships. It creates stability, transparency, and respect. There are several character traits that one must exude to display trustworthiness; authenticity, consistency, kindness, compassion, humility, openness, and availability. Are you trustworthy? Do you trust yourself?

Being fully present and engaged in your friendships demonstrate trustworthiness and commitment. Being trustworthy requires you to be thoughtful with your words by communicating with respect, empathy, and kindness. Being trustworthy requires you to be transparent, acknowledging mistakes and having a willingness to right wrongs. Being trustworthy is also having the courage to tell another woman *directly* when she has offended, hurt, or disappointed you. I stress the word "directly" because we sometimes tell everyone that we were offended except the person who offended us, which makes these situations more complex than they need to be. I am a believer in speaking directly to the source. Trustworthy friends demonstrate integrity, and they know the importance of keeping private information between friends. Gossiping is a sure way to betray a friend's trust.

"No one who gossips can be trusted with a secret, but you can put confidence in someone who is trustworthy ... a gossip can never keep a secret. Stay away from people who talk too much."

- Proverbs 11:13 and 20:19

Week 20: Prevail

What did you do this week to create more trust in your relationships? Sometimes, it's listening, being there, and refraining from judgment. Think about it and reflect below. If nothing comes to mind, consider how you'll demonstrate your trustworthiness in the days and weeks to come.

_____

_____

_____

_____

_____

_____

_____

_____

_____

_____

_____

Respect is earned.
Honesty is appreciated.
Trust is gained.
Loyalty is returned.

WEEK 21

Power Move:

Respond with an attitude of resilience when right goes wrong.

Week 21: Positioning

As long as you continue to try, you have not failed. We are faced with challenges and difficult times that can promote and position us to prevail. You are allowed to cry, pout, put yourself in time out, and scream, but you are not allowed to give up. Smile at your setbacks; every strikeout brings you closer to your next home run. Acknowledge setbacks. Allow them to sting you. Address the wounds, but do not allow them to seep into your soul! Refuse to be defined by your setbacks... we are not our mistakes; we are not our struggles! There is success on the other side of struggle.

Don't be mad about your past experiences, because experience is a good teacher. Tell yourself. "I have not failed. I've just found a few ways that didn't work." Failure is not an option. Even the most accomplished and successful women encounter setbacks sometimes. The more bitter the lessons, the greater the successes will be. The bible encourages us about these setbacks in Romans 8:28, "And we know that God causes everything to work together for the good of those who love God and are called according to his purpose for them.

Your past was never a mistake if you learned from it. So take all of the experiences and lessons learned, and place them in a box labeled "Thank you!" Will it be easy? No! Will it be worth it? Yes! I have been through more hell than anyone will ever know. Guess what? I wear that pain like a 10 carat rock on my finger, but there comes a time when we must sift through our setbacks and understand how they occurred in the first place. Was this a repeat offense on your part? You may have to fight the same battle more than once, but at least you will know what weapon to use each time. Difficult times can define who you are, diminish who you are, or develop you into the person you are destined to be. You decide!

Week 21: Prevail

Create your "Thank You!" box this week! Find a shoe box or even a small gift box. Take out some paper. On the front side, write your toughest or greatest experiences. On the back side of each piece of paper, write down the lesson learned or the revelation that you received from each experience. Fold those pieces of paper up and drop them in that box.

_____

_____

_____

_____

_____

_____

_____

_____

_____

_____

_____

"Think like a queen. A queen is not afraid to fail. Failure is another stepping stone to greatness."

- Oprah Winfrey

WEEK 22

Power Move:

Be authentic.

Week 22: Positioning

Being authentic comes from the core, deep within. Let go of others' perceptions of you and focus on God's purpose for you. Authentic people create their own rules based on the standards that resonate with them. Don't compromise who you are in order to make others comfortable around you. Be who God designed you to be and never stop trying to improve that woman. You do not have to compromise who you are or compete with another woman for what God reserved for you. Being authentic means being yourself.

Some people may not like you, but it's fine because some people are struggling to like themselves. If you listen closely, people will tell you exactly who they are before they show you… just listen. That's why we have to be quick to listen and slow to speak. Be in relationship with those who can relate, but also with those who are a bit different; hence the reason why you should diversify your partnerships. Allow people to see the real, imperfect, flawed, beautiful, magical, and powerful woman that you are.

You have to always trust yourself, think for yourself, be yourself, speak for yourself, and never give up on yourself! Watch what happens if you don't give up. The only person you should be in competition with is yourself and never stop being better than the person you were yesterday. Never send your representative... own who you are! Every day is a great day to be yourself because everyone else is taken!

Week 22: Prevail

New business owners must think about their "niche," or what sets them apart from other companies on the market. As individuals, it's wise to think about our personal niches. What are some of the traits that make you authentically you? What is it that you do differently than anyone else? How do you show up authentically each day? Write that below.

_____

_____

_____

_____

_____

_____

_____

_____

_____

_____

_____

_____

"*Never try to wear another woman's heels. You are destined to fall!*"

- Natasha M. Brown

WEEK 23

Power Move:

Self-awareness is a major key.

Week 23: Positioning

Being self-aware means that you have a sharp realization of your personality; your strengths and weaknesses; your thoughts and beliefs; your emotions; and your motivations. Being forced to see yourself as you really are is a very difficult and scary process, but making the right efforts to know your true self can be extremely rewarding. This will allow you the opportunity to improve yourself so that you can prevail in all areas of your life. We must have the desire to confront ourselves, and not others first.

Self-awareness is empowering because it arms you with knowledge and enables you to make better choices. We have the choice to soar or remain stagnate. Self-awareness is not a one-time self-assessment, but more of a series of self-observations and self-discovery.

Take the blinders off so that you can be aware of those traits or aspects about yourself that limit your growth. As you know, growth is a sure sign of maturity. Take some time out daily for intentional introspection. Think about **yourself** with a purpose. I have enjoyed getting to know myself over this past year and have fallen deeply in love with the woman I've come to know.

Powerful women have the capacity to change...

Week 23: Prevail

What are your pet-peeves?

What are your needs?

What patterns have you observed in your behavior that you want to change? Have other people made these same observations about you? Take a moment to become more self-aware of these personal character traits.

_____

_____

_____

_____

_____

_____

_____

_____

_____

"*Self Awareness*
+
Self Correction
+
Self Appreciation
=
Transformation"

- Natasha M. Brown

WEEK 24

Power Move:

If you want what you've never had, you have to do what you've never done!

Week 24: Positioning

You can't get something new by doing what you've always done, and your faith has to stand tall in the process of doing something new. Whatever your vision is for your preferred destiny, start the preparation phase. Earning a degree, pursuing a higher degree, completing a certification, finding a mentor, updating your resume, job coaching, perfecting your interviewing skills… whatever your start is, just START.

I had several "just start" moments. I recall wanting to get my master's degree, but didn't know how I was going to work a full-time job and take care of a four-year-old as a single parent. I am attracted to challenges and gave myself permission to apply for the master's program at Clark Atlanta University. On orientation day, they awarded me a $5,000 scholarship, so I knew I was following God's plan. I would work a full day as a social worker in a nursing home, pick my daughter up from daycare, stop by the gas station for a snack (she called it the restaurant), and then go to class. I was able to keep going by reminding myself that it was temporary as long as I stuck to the plan. It wasn't an ideal situation for me to take my daughter to class with me, but I reassured myself that it was all a part of the plan. And it was. I encourage you to start where you are, use what you have, do what you can… just start.

Create a mental picture of your preferred future and START. *Set true and realistic timelines;* monitor your progress; and consider forming an alliance of accountability partners. People tend to fear change because the focus is on what they have to give up to change as opposed to what they will gain by changing. Be faithful (not fearful) about your future. Fear doesn't know the strength you possess, so press your way through the struggle in order to prevail.

Week 24: Prevail

What new adventure and challenge is waiting for you to simply begin? Below, brainstorm on the plans, ambitions, and previous STARTs you've had. Which projects will you begin to execute now?

_____

_____

_____

_____

_____

_____

_____

_____

_____

_____

"The triumph can't be had without the struggle."

- **Wilma Rudolph**

WEEK 25

Power Move:

Write your own definition of success and don't allow others to define it for you.

Week 25: Positioning

The image of success is constantly being painted for us especially in this day and age of Instagram and Facebook. Someone always has something to say about what you do, how much you weigh, how independent you are or how you wear your hair. It's easy to confuse success as painted by someone else and the image of success you have inside you own heart. If you don't know what success means to you it doesn't matter how accomplished you are. It doesn't matter how successful you've been at achieving goals, you will still be empty inside.

Success takes hard work, perseverance, learning, studying, sacrifice, and most of all, doing what you love. Success is a continuous journey and doesn't stop at one accomplishment. For some, success is not about money, but more about happiness.

Success for some is about having peace of mind despite the constant chaos around them. Success could be about the difference you make in the lives of others. Take a moment to think about how you define success; write it down, and live it out. Define what success looks like for you, the real you. If that means separating yourself from others for a season so that you can hear your own thoughts, do that. Getting clear on your own vision of success is one of the most important things you can do as a successful woman.

Success for me is about a state of mind; having peace; being resilient in times of struggle; refusing to settle; living my best life; serving and sowing into others; refusing to compromise who I am and my self-worth; being intentional about my purpose; and refusing to allow anyone to place limits on my life.

Success is not what we do occasionally, it's what we do consistently. Successful people make decisions based on where they want to go, not based on their current situation. Be strategic and make your success plan sustainable. Embrace change, welcome challenges, and don't ever stop celebrating your success and the successes of others. Know the power of your mind and program it for success.

Week 25: Prevail

The time is now. Write your definition of success. What does it mean to you? How do you define it? First write your "success" definition below, then envision (in writing) an ideal day in your successful life.

Success definition

_____

_____

_____

_____

_____

A successful day looks like...

_____

_____

_____

_____

_____

"Success is liking yourself, liking what you do, and liking how you do it."

- Dr. Maya Angelou

WEEK 26

Power Move:

Crucial conversations are critical.

Week 26: Positioning

Some of us shy away from have crucial conversations for fear of conflict; however, avoiding or delaying a difficult conversation can hurt your relationships and create other negative outcomes. Unresolved conflict can cause massive damage and ultimately ruin relationships. Have the conversation with only the person involved, not the entire tribe. I am a reality TV junkie, and it burns me up when one person is ambushed by a group of women. Next thing you know, drinks are thrown. I always think about how I would react in that situation; no one is about to waste my money throwing drinks and food. Seriously, I wouldn't show up for that type of foolishness.

Crucial conversations may not feel natural at first, especially if you dread discord. Think of it from a positive perspective: a positive mindset and pure intentions can definitely result in a positive outcome. Remember, everyone reacts differently to conflict. Some people are not receptive to others' feelings and tend to be dismissive rather than being open to discussion. You can't tell someone how they are supposed to feel in any situation. Their feelings are valid.

Should this take place, know when to disengage if the conversation is no longer productive. Don't waste time trying to have a conversation with a person who is committed to misunderstanding you. The same applies if someone needs to have a crucial conversation with you. Defensiveness doesn't have a place in productive conversations, but acknowledgement will go a long way. Listen with the intent to resolve and not react. Acknowledge your faults and how you can reconcile. Always remember the importance of listening to others; truly pay attention to what people are saying or asking of you. Listen actively without making assumptions or dismissing what the other person is saying. It's difficult to discover the issue of the conflict if you're not actively listening; listen to correct the issue, not to confront.

In order to get the best out of a crucial conversation, consider the following important steps:

Ascertain whether the conversation is meant to be harmful or helpful.

Determine what you are hoping to accomplish.

Discern the best time to talk so the conversation will be well received.

Allow the other person to speak.

Avoid trigger words and blame.

Always remain poised.

Week 26: Prevail

Most people have a difficult time with conflict and crucial conversations. Think about the most recent crucial conversations you've experienced. Did these conversations end well? How are the relationships now? What would you do differently? Did you implement the steps that we mentioned on the previous page? Reflect below.

_____

_____

_____

_____

_____

_____

_____

_____

_____

_____

_____

Speak in such a way that others love to listen to you.

Listen in such a way that others love to speak to you.

WEEK 27

Power Move:

Wipe the slate clean.

Week 27: Positioning

Although the sentiment "wipe the slate clean" can be seen as such a huge task, think about how beautiful it will be to start a new day with new strength, new thoughts, and a new you. Life is messy, complicated, and chaotic. The schedule will not always go as planned. Bumps in the road are unavoidable. Unexpected situations are always going to happen, but we can't let yesterday take up too much of today. Let it go! In order to do this, you must start with a clean slate.

Imagine yourself as an artist. In order to paint a perfect picture, you must start with a clean canvas. Focus on what's before you and not why the slate was wiped clean. The blessing is this: God gives us a new day, every day. Welcome the happiness of a brand new day. Being able to wipe the slate clean shows your strength, power, and resilience. Let go of everything that is too heavy to carry forward and start fresh. Never underestimate the power of a "redo." Take some time and do some soul searching and think about how you would have done things differently if you could go back and do it again. In doing so, it will help to affirm that you have not only learned from your past mistakes, but that you would have done things differently had you had the skills you possess now, back then.

We get attached when we've invested a lot of time in something. But an investment is only as valuable as its return—meaning we owe it to ourselves to recognize we can have something better by wiping the slate clean and starting over. Trust me; I know it's not easy. In fact, it's absolutely scary, but snatch your power back and tell yourself, "I got this!" God has not brought you this far to leave you. Starting over allows you a chance to build something better the next time. Cancel the reminders of the past unless you are using those reminders as motivation for the future. Your past is what it is… your past. It's behind you.

Week 27: Prevail

To "Prevail" this week, take out a piece of paper. Write down those strong-holds or past memories that have held you or your loved ones back. Go to the backyard or use a fireplace or a paper shredder, and bury that piece of paper. It's over now. It's time to prevail.

"*Mistakes are a fact of life. It is the response to the error that counts.*"

- **Nikki Giovanni**

WEEK 28

Power Move:

Quality vs. Quantity:
Value the friendships you have over
the amount of friends you have.

Week 28: Positioning

The idea of choosing quality over quantity is not about having less, but about having more of what matters most. Great relationships have nothing to do with the frequency of contact and time spent with people. It's more about having quality friends who are solid as a rock, built tough, sustainable through good and bad circumstances, and who are resilient.

Focus on quality relationships rather than lots of relationships. This is not about closing yourself off to new people, but more so about allowing relationships to develop organically. It is about recognizing your limitations, learning to let go, and nurturing what you have. For me, it was draining and toxic to have relationships that did not energize me and instead caused me to exert more energy than they gave. Valuing substance certainly makes you find a life that's deeper and richer and yes, happier. Maintaining relationships requires time, attention, and energy. Each of us only has so much time, attention, and energy to give. Obviously, there is a limit to how many relationships we can manage well. Letting go of those toxic relationships was the most crucial step to securing my peace. I had to learn to disconnect and disengage.

Powerful women should always have a few trustworthy, valuable, well-rounded, accountable, supportive friends who inspire and motivate in their arsenal. Take the time to audit your arsenals and look for quality indicators in your friendships. If the friends you value aren't of quality, consider canceling their friendship subscriptions.

Week 28: Prevail

We've reflected a lot on the relationships, circumstances, and duties in our lives. You are more than halfway through the year now. Instead of evaluating your friendships in this space, think about the value you are adding to your relationships. What value do you bring to the five closest friendships in your life?

_____

_____

_____

_____

_____

How do you nurture your relationships as a mom, sister, aunt, and/or daughter on a daily basis?

_____

_____

_____

_____

_____

"Sometimes your circle decreases in size but increases in value."

- Natasha M. Brown

WEEK 29

Power Move:

Focus on character verses credentials.

Week 29: Positioning

Character is perhaps the most important essence a person can possess as it defines who you are. Character is permanent; credentials are transient. Many people rely on their credentials to get a position which is understandable because that is what we are taught. Credentials can get you in the door, character keeps you there!

Your character is built and tested through experiences. Trust me. Your character will certainly be tested; especially when no one is looking. On my journey to become not only a resilient woman, but a woman of good character, I realized the importance of having a solid squad of women who also have good character.

These women of character are examples of hope, courage, honesty, integrity, and favor. God will give you opportunities to grow in character as you walk through this life. He certainly did for my girlfriends and me. Are you familiar with the phenomenal women below?

Sarah, a woman of hope: She wasn't always perfect, yet she became the mother of our faith in what seemed like a hopeless situation. (See the Bible book of Genesis, chapters eleven through twenty-two).

Ruth, a woman of character: She was a widow, yet instead of putting her own needs first, she dedicated her life to serving her mother-in-law (positioning) and was rewarded in the process. (See the Bible book of Ruth).

Esther, a woman of courage: She could have died for boldly approaching the king without an invitation, yet she positioned herself spiritually through fasting and prayer and found the courage she needed to prevail. (See the Bible book of Esther).

Mary, a woman of favor: She was a virgin, yet she became the mother of our Savior; her favor shows us that nothing is impossible with God (See the Bible book of Luke 1:37).

A woman of good character takes responsibility for her life. She knows that she will make mistakes along the way and accepts that she will be wrong at times. She doesn't think that anybody owes her anything, and she works hard to make her way in the world. She doesn't want a free pass. A woman of good character treats others well and speaks well of people. She has integrity and humility and is not self-absorbed. She has common sense, is compassionate, considerate, and has the credentials to match.

Week 29: Prevail

Credentials may get you in the door, but character will keep you there. What are some character building tests that you've faced in the past, and how did they transform you? I want you to reflect on some moments that have shaped your character. In order to prevail, you will no doubt face other monumental moments that will make or break you—your character will determine the outcome.

_____

_____

_____

_____

_____

_____

_____

_____

_____

_____

Watch your thoughts, for they become words.

Watch your words, for they become actions.

Watch your actions, for they become habits.

Watch your habits, for they become character.

Watch your character, for it becomes your destiny.

WEEK 30

Power Move:

Wise women learn to leverage
their waiting seasons!

Week 30: Positioning

Learning to leverage your waiting season allows you to be better prepared for your season of increase. There will be some failing moments during your preparation season, but it is OK, because that's where you will begin to exercise your faith. You will also begin to see your distractions: what you may be doing wrong, what you can improve... and you will be able to discern the people who can handle you in your preparation season. During this time, God will do a mighty work in you. He will show you some things about you that you didn't know existed. He will show you that you have more strength than you thought, and in that season, you may notice your strength begin to intimidate those around you. Could it be that your strength reveals their weaknesses?

Think about Esther in the Bible. Before this young woman's turn came to go in to see King Xerxes, she had to complete twelve months of beauty treatments prescribed for the women, six months with oil of myrrh, and six with perfumes and cosmetics." (Esther 2:12) We read further that, "Esther won the favor of everyone who saw her," (Esther 2:15). When she finally had her turn (and possibly the only turn) with the King, we read that, "The king loved Esther more than all the women, and she obtained grace and favor in his sight more than all the maidens, so that he set the royal crown on her head and made her queen instead of Vashti," (Esther 2:17).

Can you imagine one shot with the king after a twelve month waiting period? Honestly ask yourself, if you had that one shot right now would you be ready?

Your faith will go to a whole new level during your preparation phase. Faith is the substance of things hoped for and the evidence of things unseen. You have to prepare for the next season before it happens. While you are in the preparation phase, meditate on what the Word of God says in

Philippians 4:6, "Don't be anxious about anything, but in every situation, by prayer and petition, with thanksgiving, present your requests to God." We can't present our requests then have a breakdown, stress out, and try to work them out by ourselves. Have peace in knowing that what you pray and prepare for will come to past at the set time, because wise women learn to leverage their waiting seasons! Tell yourself and God this: "I don't mind waiting!"

Week 30: Prevail

What are you waiting and preparing for? Write what's on your wait list and then write a personal note of commitment to yourself identifying how you will prepare during this season. Pray for God's grace and strength.

Wait List

_____

_____

_____

_____

_____

I'm preparing by

_____

_____

_____

_____

_____

_____

"*Never be afraid to sit awhile and think.*"

- **Lorraine Hansberry**

POSITIONED TO PREVAIL

WEEK 31

Power Move:

Powerful women don't operate
in the unknown.
Ask, don't assume.

Week 31: Positioning

One of the biggest ways people handicap themselves today is by being too afraid to ask questions. There is plenty of knowledge all around us to be gained. The unfortunate side effect of not asking enough questions is poor decision-making. That's why it's imperative that we slow down and take the time to ask more and better questions. Asking questions is a sign of strength and intelligence – not a sign of weakness or uncertainty. Powerful women constantly ask questions and are well aware that they do not have all the answers. The answers we think we know could be wrong.

There is danger in making assumptions. Assumptions can cause missed opportunities and misunderstandings. Assuming could very well cause us to cancel people out of our lives because we assumed and didn't take the time to ask. A lot of damage can be done by confusing our assumptions with our perceptions. We have to be careful not to allow fear to keep us from asking questions for clarification because assumptions can set you up to suffer and cause you to miss your next opportunity for success. God said in Matthew 7:7, "Ask and it shall be given to you, seek and ye shall find..." ask questions and seek answers if you are unsure.

Whether it be at work, with your family, or friends...ask, and don't assume, in order to gain a better appreciation of the issues. Gain clarity by asking questions. Intelligent questions stimulate, provoke, inform, and inspire.

Constantly ask questions and be vulnerable enough to know you do not have all the answers. We need to rely on the knowledge of others around us especially if they have the answers. The most educated people in the world never stop learning or look down on someone with a desire to learn. When we think we know, we cancel out the opportunity to learn.

Week 31: Prevail

What questions do you need to ask, and of whom, to move confidently into your next season of life?

_____

_____

_____

_____

_____

_____

_____

_____

_____

_____

She who is afraid to ask questions is afraid to learn.

WEEK 32

Power Move:

You have the power to change your mind.

Week 32: Positioning

As I approached forty, I knew there were several things I was going to have to change in order for me to be at peace and to have a healthy state of mind. One morning, I woke up different and it was in this moment that I realized my new year didn't have to start on January 1. It would start on the day I decided to change my mind for better.

I was in a position for over five years, and yet I was not growing. The environment was toxic. The women were unprofessional, and there were no opportunities for growth. The flip side of this was an attractive benefits package, travel, and the ability to telecommute. I could take my daughters to work if necessary and taking time off was never an issue. I had to realize that I had become complacent, which led to comfortability, and then I started to conform because I feared change. I was losing brain cells daily. You know that *if you don't use it you will lose it.* Every time I thought about changing jobs, I panicked. Remembering the three Cs caused a shift in my thinking: Choices. Chances. Changes. You must make a choice to take a chance or you will never change. This truth was always in the back of my mind.

Change is vital to make progress in life; it may be painful, but nothing is as painful than an unchanged mind. You've heard the old saying, "The mind is a terrible thing to waste." Our minds are weapons, so we must be careful how we use them. One reason people resist change is because they focus on what they have to give up instead of what they have to gain. Progress is impossible without change, and those who cannot change their minds cannot change anything. Start small: notice your mistakes, and work to change them.

I wasted a lot of time clinging to things that had run their course. I am proud of myself for every single decision I have made, every change for the better, and for changing my priorities. Life begins at the end of the comfort zone. Be a world changer...you have the power to change your mind. Welcome to today, another day for another chance to change.

Week 32: Prevail

Remembering the three Cs caused a shift in my thinking: Choices. Chances. Changes. You must make a choice to take a chance or you will never change. This truth was always in the back of my mind.

What important **choice** are you facing today?

_____

_____

_____

What **chances** or opportunities are you faced with?

_____

_____

_____

What **change** can these decisions lead to?

_____

_____

_____

"Change can either challenge or cripple you have the power to decide!"

- Natasha M. Brown

WEEK 33

Power Move:

Your willingness to make sacrifices determines your level of success.

Week 33: Positioning

Life is all about choices; you get to decide what you're willing to give up in order to gain what you cherish most. Sometimes, it requires a change in lifestyle or a willingness to start over again. Be sure to give every sacrifice careful consideration. Sometimes, it means letting go of accomplishments or positions that you've already worked so hard to achieve and recognizing that you still have a lot to learn. Sacrifice requires you to release the fears that have prevented you from taking your life to the next level.

What you value most can be determined by what you are willing to sacrifice. Ask yourself these questions:

What am I willing to sacrifice in order to grow?

What am I willing to release now to get closer to my future goals?

Ask yourself the hard questions and make the hard decisions when you think the time is right.

Recognize that in every opportunity for growth, something is gained and something else is lost. There's nothing wrong with it, though. That's the cycle of life. There are so many sacrifices I had to make in my lifetime. I've had to pass up vacations because I needed to save money to buy a home. I've had to forego girls' nights out and dinners, and I even sold my home to move into a two-bedroom apartment that was very uncomfortable for my family. This however was all a part of the plan that I had. I needed my girls to be in a better school district. I moved from Mobile, Alabama to Atlanta, Georgia to make a better living for myself...only making one dollar more than I was making in Mobile. The struggle was very real for me, but guess what?

My struggle was the pathway to my success! I knew one day what appeared to be huge sacrifices would yield the greatest return on my investment. Just like it was for me, the only person who can determine whether or not any sacrifice is worthwhile is YOU.

Week 33: Prevail

Weeks ago, you defined "success" according to your own standards. Today, determine what you are willing to sacrifice, or better yet, what are you being called to sacrifice now in order to achieve the "success" you've defined for yourself? Don't leave this blank. Every level of success requires a sacrifice.

_____

_____

_____

_____

_____

_____

_____

_____

_____

_____

You owe it to yourself
to sacrifice
for your future.

WEEK 34

Power Move:

Stop ignoring the warning signs...
PAY ATTENTION.

Week 34: Positioning

Stop ignoring the warning signs… PAY ATTENTION. My inspiration for this Power Move came as a result of being stranded on the side of the road, in 5 o'clock traffic, on a FRIDAY, in ATLANTA, on Interstate 85! If you live in Atlanta, you know the struggle.

I was in a rental, a Nissan Pathfinder…When I started driving away from the office, I had my music blasting, thinking about going to get my hair shampooed, and making plans for afterwards. After a few minutes of driving, I saw "warning" flashing on the dashboard, but I didn't know what that meant since I was in an unfamiliar car. I kept driving, because this was a 2018 Nissan Pathfinder, so clearly nothing could be wrong with it. Plus, I had an important appointment to make. As I merged onto the interstate, with my music blasting, singing at the top of lungs, I felt a sudden jerk. The SUV started slowing down, and my heart skipped several beats. In that moment, I realized I couldn't see the gas needle because the steering wheel obstructed my view.

Once I sat up to look over the steering wheel, I realized I was out of gas! Believe it or not, I did not get upset, yell obscenities, or cry. I sat there for a minute and reflected on this very statement: "Had I just paid attention to the warning sign!" In that moment, I thought about all of the warning signs God gave me in the past, but my view was obstructed. I looked over what I thought were pebbles when they were life-altering problems—mountains designed to keep me at a standstill. We have to take the blinders off so we don't miss the wisdom in the warnings.

This was a teachable moment for me, and I refused to give the devil credit when God was trying to tell me something. The lesson is simply this: stop being in such a hurry to get to the destination that you miss the warning signs that were placed in plain sight. We have these plans for our lives and details about how we are going to achieve them, but God can care less about our plans because they are ours and not HIS. I have learned to allow God to interrupt my plans because I trust God enough to know He has something better in store for me. He already knows what's best for me, so why in the world would I try to change God's trajectory for my life. If you are anything like me, you need every detail, but in this new season, God has told me to just go with it, enjoy the journey. *I am doing a new thing, just be ready to move when I tell you to move!* God will fill us in and involve us when necessary, but don't ignore His warning signs.

Week 34: Prevail

This week's "Prevail" may or may not require you to journal, but I challenge you to dig deep and search the hidden warning signs that could be in plain sight. What could God be trying to warn you about? Has anything odd happened? Have you written off anything or circumstance that could be a warning? Pray about it and reflect below if necessary.

_____

_____

_____

_____

_____

_____

_____

_____

_____

"Ignoring the warning signs is a sure way to end up at the wrong destination."

-Natasha M. Brown

WEEK 35

Power Move:

Forgive yourself for past faults.

Week 35: Positioning

The "fault" that has hurt me the most is feeling like I have robbed both of my girls the opportunity to be raised in households with their fathers. Not only that, but they have different fathers. When people would ask questions or make comments such as, "What are their last names, because I know they're different?" I would make light of the situation and respond, "Yes, girl you know I am a statistic!" I have tried my best to make sure the girls never felt neglected no matter what they saw in other households. Grasping the concept of blended families and positive co-parenting has also helped me on this journey of forgiveness. I never wanted to look back or have to explain to my girls why they didn't get to spend time with their fathers. I always made it a point to never speak negatively about their fathers to them and never robbed them or their fathers of the opportunity to spend time together. I wanted to show them that no matter what, I could have a positive relationship with their fathers. I realized they wouldn't experience certain moments, like, "Go ask your daddy." Instead, it is, "Call and ask your daddy." I have learned to make the sweetest glass of lemonade with all the lemons life has gifted to me.

I had to forgive myself for the choices I made because those choices provided me the chance to experience being a mother. It may not have been in the way I had imagined, but I wouldn't trade my past, because without these experiences, I wouldn't be properly and powerfully positioned. Being a single mother has certainly helped me achieve resilience. I had to apologize repeatedly to God for the days when I felt like giving up and didn't recognize that He had already given me the strength to endure. God will not allow us to go through the pain without allowing us to experience the greater good of the pain. Hear me clearly. We will go through things that don't seem fair. We won't be able to alter them, but we will be able to advance and achieve the promises God has in store.

The reason I've felt so much guilt and shame for my actions was because those actions were not in line with my morals and values. I had to turn the page and accept those actions as part of my story, and I challenge you to do the same. They've all contributed to making us who we are. Gratefulness for those experiences allows you to move on and truly forgive yourself. The process will be different for everyone, but we have to forgive and move forward. Forgiveness (for me) was a process, and it didn't happen overnight. You are more than your past mistakes, and I promise you, you are so worth your promises!

Week 35: Prevail

In this space, rewrite your story. Forgive yourself for the past and focus on the amazing qualities your past has provided you for the future. List those qualities below.

_____

_____

_____

_____

_____

_____

_____

_____

_____

_____

_____

_____

Love yourself.
Be true to yourself.
Forgive yourself.

"Forgiveness is a gift you can give to yourself."

- Suzanne Somers

WEEK 36

Power Move:

I may be bruised, but I'm not broken.

Week 36: Positioning

Webster defines broken as having been fractured or damaged and no longer in one piece; having given up all hope; despair. A bruise is an injury transmitted through unbroken skin to underlying tissue. Please reflect on the difference between the two: broken is no longer in one piece; bruised is unbroken skin.

You will be faced with some situations that will rock your world, but you cannot break! We are strong, we are resilient, and God has built each of us to withstand the bruises. We all get bruised, but you have to care for the bruise the same way you care for minor scrapes; rinse them off, apply some ointment, put a BAND-AID® on them, or simply let the bruises breathe and heal naturally.

I've been (what I thought was) broken many times—through illness, the loss of a job, through the derailment of a dream, and through the death of my mother. It wasn't until I had a near fatal car accident in 2009 that I started to look at "broken" in a different light. The doctors didn't think I would make it, and the neurologist told me my brain would not function fully again. The cuts were so deep they eventually left keloids. I eventually consulted with a cosmetic surgeon because the keloids made me a bit uncomfortable when I wore sleeveless tops. The surgeon explained all of my options for surgery but he was uncertain if the keloids would come back.

I took some time to think about my options, and in that moment, I reflected on how God brought me through a traumatic car accident. I realized that some people don't live to tell the story… people like my mom. I looked at my scars in the mirror and told myself from that moment on I would look at those scars as my battle bruises, because I went to battle with a tractor trailer and won.

I am confident that since I survived that experience, I can survive whatever battle is placed before me. I found the beauty in my bruises, and so can you… Bruises are evidence of resilience.

Build yourself from the bruises you have sustained in life. Find your strength and snatch your power.

YOU ARE STRONG and UNBREAKABLE!

Week 36: Prevail

What has happened that intended to break you, but simply bruised you instead? Share those moments below along with the lessons they taught you.

_____

_____

_____

_____

_____

_____

_____

_____

_____

_____

_____

_____

"Never allow anything or anyone to break your resilience. Resolve to be resilient."

- Natasha M. Brown

WEEK 37

Power Move:

Your image is incredibly important.

Week 37: Positioning

I am on a mission to help women represent themselves well in every aspect of their lives, especially in the workplace. Image has become incredibly important. In an instant, image can convey so much, such as one's level of success, status, character, personality, and of course, style. Whether you like it or not, people will form an opinion about you before they even know you, solely based on what you are wearing and how you carry yourself.

A well-dressed woman tends to stand out. Perception is often reality. What you wear not only communicates who you are in the minds of others, but also influences how others may interact with you. Research shows that your appearance strongly influences other people's perception of your financial success, authority, trustworthiness, intelligence, and suitability for hire or promotion. Your image is one of the most basic aspects of you, that you can not only manage, but change for yourself.

Dressing well is an act of self-love. It shows that you respect and care about yourself. If shopping and putting together outfits is not your strong suit, consider investing in an image consultant. An image consultant shows you how to find clothes that fit properly, flatter your body, and will help you pull together a wardrobe that works for you and not against you.

I wear my clothing as armor for situations. When I have a big meeting or presentation, I wear what makes me feel how I want to be perceived; chic and powerful. My goal is to command the room without speaking, and for my audience to take me seriously.

No matter where you are on the organizational chart, you represent the company you work for and your attire is a significant part of that image. No matter what, always ensure your image is impressive. Don't make excuses for not dressing appropriately. When you dress yourself, glance in the mirror, and try to see yourself from the perspective of a boss or a customer. How would you feel about doing business with someone dressed in a similar manner?

Week 37: Prevail

For a moment, think about the woman whose image has impressed you the most. Consider the aspects of her outer appearance that made her impressive. How was her body language and posture? How did her clothes fit? What was her hair like and how did she speak? Describe her below. Is that woman you, and if not, what have you learned about her image that you may want to adopt for yourself?

_____

_____

_____

_____

_____

_____

_____

_____

_____

_____

"*Style is a way to say who you are without having to speak.*"

- **Rachel Zoe**

WEEK 38

Power Move:

Stay ready so you don't have
to get ready!

Week 38: Positioning

We know that life is unpredictable and seemingly random at times, and there are many situations that take us by surprise that we never see coming or that we can't prepare for. Practicing the art of preparation positions you to be ready for whatever comes your way.

I absolutely love to entertain and have friends over. Years ago, my friend would tell me I never had two items that actually matched. I would have jelly, but no peanut butter, ketchup but no mustard, black pepper, no salt, sandwich meat, without bread. I was young and only purchased items I needed. I didn't make a grocery list, and I had to constantly run to the store every time I needed something. This was draining, and one day I woke up different and knew I needed to organize my life better. I feel all sorts of anxiety if my home is not organized. That goes beyond cleanliness even though that is important.

Do you ever find yourself having to go to the mall whenever there's an event, having to make multiple trips to the grocery store, rushing to clean the house whenever someone is coming over? My mom taught me this as a child, "Don't come out of the house without your face and earrings on and a gift to give; make your bed daily, and make sure that the kitchen and bathroom are always clean because you never know who will have to bring you home!" She also taught me to always have something in the refrigerator to offer guests because you never know who God may send to be fed.

Just as there are staple items we should shop for like milk, bread and eggs, there are a few items that every woman should keep in her arsenal. These items include a simple black dress, black suit, white shirt, plain black pumps, plain jeans, simple white t-shirt, statement necklace, and simple earrings.

Take a moment to consider how you go about your daily life. Are you missing out on some wonderful opportunities because you resist preparation?

Week 38: Prevail

Sometimes without even realizing it, we are our own worst enemies. It may have seemed like the position, relationship, or opportunity was evading you, but perhaps it's been the other way around. Are you ready for everything you've been praying for, desiring, or expecting? Be honest with yourself, and use the space below to evaluate yourself and decide if you are truly prepared and positioned to prevail in the areas you desire.

_____

_____

_____

_____

_____

_____

_____

_____

_____

_____

WEEK 39

Power Move:

Your words have power,
use them wisely.

Week 39: Positioning

It is true: the tongue is small but can do enormous damage. I have caused the damage and have been damaged by what someone has said to me. It's easy to say something that will hurt someone and stay in his or her mind for months—something that will greatly impact that person's future. Words have the power to build people up or break them down. That is why we're supposed to be careful with what we say to someone else because we never know how it will be interpreted or how long they will replay those words in their minds. I recall the saying, "Before you speak, let your words pass through the three gates: Is it true, is it necessary, is it kind?"

Just because we can't see the wounds of our words doesn't mean they aren't literally and physically there. You might be honest and correct, but the "truth" may still hurt feelings, hence the reason why we should humble our opinions. Consider the effect words may have on others, and adjust your words accordingly. I have learned the hard way, and my new motto is, "Everything that needs to be said doesn't have to be said by me." I got tired of being the one to speak up first and by trying to correct the situation, sure enough, I would end up in some form of conflict. Sometimes, it is better to be silent and smile. Those are two powerful weapons. Smiling solves problems and silence is the way to avoid problems.

Week 39: Prevail

Think about the power your words have had on your life. Follow the prompts below.

Share a time when your words had a powerful effect in a situation:

_____

_____

_____

What big takeaways can you pinpoint about your communication in that situation?

_____

_____

_____

Recall a time when your words led to conflict:

_____

_____

_____

What are your takeaways from the situation?

_____

_____

_____

What are some key adjectives that describe how you want to communicate and how you want to be known (in regards to your communication/dealings with others)?

_____

_____

_____

How will you make sure the above desires become a reality?

_____

_____

_____

"I've learned that people will forget what you said, people will forget what you did, but people will never forget how you made them feel."

- Dr. Maya Angelou

WEEK 40

Power Move:

Say "Thank you."

Week 40: Positioning

For me, "thank you" is one of the most powerful word combinations. "Thank you" is so simple and effective, but people often forget it… This is one of the first lessons we learn as children because some situations require an expression of gratitude and humility. I can recall being offered candy at church or a lollipop at the bank as a child.

My mom would say, "Use your manners. What do you say?" I would reply, "Thank you." How have we lost the art of saying "thank you" as adults? My mom raised my two brothers and I. There were times when she needed to apply for community resources to have our utility bill paid so the power wouldn't get turned off. We would have to arrive at the place called Community Action for public assistance in the wee hours of the morning to be first in line. My mom would drop me off to stand in the line while she worked a few hours, and when I got close to the front, I would call her to come.

Every time the case worker approved my mom (no matter how often we needed this assistance), my mom would cry and tell her "thank you," but she didn't stop there. My mom would go home and bake our case worker a pound cake. She would send me to take the cake and instruct me to say, "This is the least my mom could do to thank you for helping our family." You best believe that caseworker looked out for mom every time, and made sure she received funds every time, simply because of my mom's gratitude.

In life, there have always been ungrateful people, but this doesn't mean that we are all ungrateful. We must be careful not to criticize before we compliment, especially when someone is doing something out of the kindness of their hearts. Try not to miss the opportunity to say "thank you" to those who are providing a service to you, coordinating an event, or extending an invitation.

In the midst of our busy lives, we text and email out of convenience and look for those three dots (if you're an iPhone user), hoping for a quick response. Once we receive the response, we quickly move on to the next task. Often, our focus was on the response, and we forget that the person just provided a service. Saying "thank you" is so powerful in that it makes people more willing to do something for you again in the future.

Sadly, most of us are simply not using this very potent, little, two-word sentence as effectively as we could be. While some say this may be old-fashioned, in my book, a thank you note or letter will never go out of style. The biggest advantage is that the recipient can read it again and again and again. It also shows your sincere appreciation and gratitude for their act of service. The hardest heart may be healed by a simple, but sincere, "thank you." My mom also told me that people don't have to be kind, so when they are, thank them. Have an attitude of gratitude.

Week 40: Prevail

It's **Gratitude Journal Day!** Write everything that you are thankful for today. This teaches us to appreciate what we have, and we develop a posture of humility with each act of thankfulness. How many people can you think of who you can thank that you may have overlooked in the past? Who can you think of that you can thank again with more passion? Who will you always remember to thank in the future? Allow your thoughts to flow below.

_____

_____

_____

_____

_____

_____

_____

_____

_____

The most powerful words in any language are "thank you."

WEEK 41

Power Move:

Learn to hear the voice of God.

Week 41: Positioning

It is so important to still your spirit in order to hear from God. I was going through so many rough phases in my life, and I felt like I couldn't catch a break. I was afraid to be alone because I wanted to avoid thinking about how jacked up I really was. I couldn't understand who God was to me and allow Him to show Himself to me because I was always in a crowd. But when GOD got me by myself, I felt a shaking in my spirit. I heard a soft voice say, "I got you now!" I was able to see the sovereignty of God's presence in my life, and I discovered the worth of Natasha.

Think about it like this... When you allow God to reveal himself to you and learn to hear his voice, you are then able to discern God's best for you. Ladies, this is real for me. If we can't hear from God, we will settle for anything. We will never know what will suit us if we don't allow God to speak it to us. We look for what looks good, sounds good, and feels comfortable, and we settle. Then we turn temporary situations into permanent solutions, and we stay stuck.

One thing I know for sure, God is not going to bless some mess, especially when He threw smoke signals, warning signs, and messages in a bottle. We must be careful not to look for answers in people, because people will try to hold you in their own personal prisons. Answers are found in your instincts and that's the very place where God will increase you. Think about when you go in the store to shop for something and the sales associate asks, "Can I help you find something?" You respond, "I will know it when I see it!" When you find it, you say, "That's the one right there." That's called instinct.

God wants to be our own personal GPS system, using our instincts to navigate us through life. The blessing of this is just like when we make a wrong turn while driving, the GPS guides us to the next safest location, and tells us to make a U-turn. That's exactly how God deals with us. Stay off the phone, quiet yourself, because God wants to speak to you and through your present situation. Have no fear, because God is for you! You can't fear because God has called you to walk by faith.

I always pray for God to reveal his perfect will... not permissive will, for my life. Then I wait patiently, because I will know when the answer is from God. The clues are in my instincts, and the feeling I get when making the decision. I'll let you in on another secret about me. I start sweating so bad when I get anxiety about a situation. That's God telling me to go sit myself down somewhere! Your instincts are found in the voice of God, which is why it's important to still your spirit in order to hear from HIM. He will not fail you nor forsake you, because He wants the best for you. Don't override the voice of God. Have peace in knowing better is before you.

Week 41: Prevail

Quiet yourself. Take out your journal (or use the space below). Practice two-way journaling: write what God is saying to you. Pray before you begin, "Lord, I want to hear from you about this situation [be specific]." Write what God is saying to you.

_____

_____

_____

_____

_____

_____

_____

_____

_____

_____

"Trust your instincts. Intuition doesn't lie."

- Natasha M. Brown

WEEK 42

Power Move:

Self-care is not selfish.

Week 42: Positioning

What would happen if you treated yourself the same way that you treat your best friend, husband, children, boyfriend, or job? You would be more attuned to your needs, your problems, and your goals. So many women constantly put everyone else first while allowing their own needs to suffer.

In 2016, I heard the phrase "self-care" for the first time. I was in a casual setting with a group of friends, and we were having a conversation about our busy lives, hectic schedules, and children's activities. A woman with us repeatedly said, "self-care." I thought *I do take care of myself. I get my hair shampooed weekly, I take showers, I am well dressed, sure, I could stand to lose a few pounds, but...* I was confused by what she meant by self-care. When I connected with Licensed Clinical Psychologist Dr. RJ on social media, I saw her post about self-care, but it wasn't until I listened to her radio show that I began to understand what it truly meant.

Dr. RJ says, "It's in our DNA to run ourselves on empty! We have to be conscious and aware when we are not taking care of self, it is essential to our survival!" She goes on to state that, "Self-care is foreign to women of color. Neglecting ourselves and constantly running on fumes can lead to panic attacks, heart attacks, and other illnesses."

It became clear to me that I didn't take care of myself very well, and as a result, I always felt empty. I was emotionally incapacitated. Some women may even become resentful because their personal needs have been neglected. Neglecting ourselves causes us to overlook when we are hurting. Whether it be a death or divorce, our hearts need to be healed. Women who do not take this precious time to care for their hearts will lose as soon as they gain, because their hearts have not healed. Change the trajectory of your life by taking control of your emotional health. If this can't be done independently, consider therapy as an option.

Allow yourself to be emotionally unavailable until you fall in love with yourself all over again. This won't happen while you're trying to fix everything for everyone. You will eventually experience burnout by signing up for other people's drama. Self-care allows you to be more generous to yourself, as you are to others. Start by placing yourself at the top of your "to do" list and learn the importance of SELF!

Week 42: Prevail

Below brainstorm on all of the ways that you take care of yourself and the parts of yourself that these activities will support.

Self-Care Activity   Helps me with...

_____

_____

_____

_____

_____

_____

_____

_____

_____

_____

"Make YOUR self-care the first priority in your life."

- Natasha M. Brown

WEEK 43

Power Move:

Always strive to make progress…
progression is pivotal for powerful women.

Week 43: Positioning

You are not under any obligation to be the same person you were yesterday or even right before you read this devotion. We tend to get complacent in our comfort zones, but staying in that place will eventually cripple you. You have the right to progress and don't ever apologize for growing. Give yourself permission to proceed in a new direction. Free your mind, free yourself of murmuring, and free yourself of misery. People may say you have changed, and your response should be, "I did," and don't allow them to hold you hostage to your past. As you progress to your next level, people may walk away. Let them walk!

Allow God to shut doors in your life that were not meant to be open, and don't cry over closed doors because God will open another one. You must have confidence in knowing that God has a bigger and better door ready for you to open. Your destiny is waiting. There were places you used to go and people who you dealt with when those doors were open that you can't have in your life in your new season. Look in your rear view mirror for motivation as you progress to the next level. Appreciate the small steps along the way. Throw your own "progress party..." table for one, please! There will be pitfalls as you progress, but push your way through. We know what "PUSH" really means, right? Pray Until Something Happens. Be specific, be strategic, and be serious about what you pray for. Not every day will be a good day, but show up anyway. Wake up with purpose and intent in your heart and mind. When you feel like giving up, think about the reason why you started.

Use your personal prison to your advantage, and seek God for his perfect plan for your life. Refocus, re-adjust, re-calibrate, reset, and have a prison break! I have veered off course so many times, BUT God still comes back to grab my hand and guides me back. I never changed the plan, just the process. Position yourself to progress in every area of your life whether it be parenting, marriage, friendships, career, etc., because your destiny awaits.

Remember, perfection does not exist, but progression does.

Week 43: Prevail

What are you PUSHing for?

_____

_____

_____

_____

Do you have any prisons that you need to break from?

_____

_____

_____

_____

In what area are you praying for the biggest progress?

_____

_____

_____

_____

Whenever I feel bad, I use that feeling to motivate me to work harder. I only allow myself one day to feel sorry for myself. When I'm not feeling my best, I ask myself, 'What are you gonna do about it?' I use the negativity to fuel the transformation into a better me."

— **Beyoncé**

WEEK 44

Power Move:

Lead in all aspects of your life.

Week 44: Positioning

Having the courage to step up and lead is tied to your commitment for the cause. Having a willingness to step up to do the hard work provides the opportunity to increase your own level of leadership. Leading is hard work and heart work; even exhausting work, but someone has to take the lead. Why not let it be you? Some women are afraid to lead because they don't want to be in the front but leading doesn't always require you to be in the limelight. Leaders may be behind the scenes or in the back of the line working because there are different levels of leadership.

You may be afraid of leading due to fear of making important decisions. Girlfriend, even the best leaders make bad decisions sometimes. Avoiding a decision is always the worst move. Leadership has taught me that you're going to be criticized no matter what (by some) and accepted no matter what by others. The ones who are first to complain about those in leadership are the very ones who were afraid to commit due to their fear of leadership. Sadly, they probably didn't realize that they also had it in them to lead. FEAR is hindering them. Don't you dare be afraid to take the lead because you don't want to become a target for criticism. Criticism builds character. I get it; you're making yourself responsible for the potentially negative outcomes of your decisions. All leaders will experience successes and opportunities for improvement when making decisions that affect others. It's all a part of growing and learning.

Leadership is not tied to the number of degrees you have either. Some women have fewer educational credentials, but hold higher positions because of their ability to lead. They are bold and unafraid of new challenges. God is going to equip you with the qualities you need to lead especially if that is what you have been called to do. He knows what you need before you know what you need. We are already leaders; we lead our families and households daily.

Give yourself the opportunity to lead and be fearless in your approach. Consider this week a strategic intervention. It is time for you to TAKE THE LEAD.

Week 44: Prevail

You can and should lead in every area of your life. Below, create a strategy to become a better leader in your various roles.

Spiritual

Family

Career

Personal Life

Friendships

Finances

_____

_____

_____

_____

_____

_____

"We need to reshape our own perceptions of how we view ourselves. We have to step up and take the lead."

– Beyoncé

POSITIONED TO PREVAIL

WEEK 45

Power Move:

Your morning determines your day.

Week 45: Positioning

The morning is usually the only time of the day when we take care of ourselves well. After that, we as women, become focused on taking care of everyone and everything else. If you begin your morning on a high note, you have a better chance at having a powerful and productive day.

What was your first thought upon waking today? Were you in a great mood, ready to get your day started? Were you grateful just to wake up? Were you in a bad mood due to lack of sleep or dreading a task? I always try to start my day on a high note by preparing the night before. I prep lunches, lay out clothes, settle my home by 9 p.m., and quiet my spirit. My mornings are pretty high energy; devotion, music blasting and singing loudly. I must admit, I check my phone as soon as I wake up. This became a habit after I missed the call from the hospital when my mom passed away. I thank God, and then peek my head down the hall to make sure I see my daughter's bathroom light on, which tells me she's up and moving. My morning is such a routine. I know that my youngest should be walking into my bathroom at a certain time to say, "Good morning, Mommy!"

For years, my daughters and I have had the same morning prayer that we say together, "Lord thank you for waking us up this morning and starting us on our way in our right minds and good health. Guide us, guard us and protect us all the day long, and be gracious unto us. Wrap your loving arms around us, keep us from all harm and danger, protect our families and friends, protect our going out and our coming in. In Jesus' name. Amen." Then we each say a specific prayer. Once we arrive at the school, I always say, "Be your best self!" to my youngest.

Sending them off to school in a bad mood would affect their learning and how they interact with other kids. I am by no means trying to sound like the perfect mom or supermom, because I am far from that, but having a morning routine that's high energy helps my family, and it can help you, too!

You decide how your day goes and if you start it joyfully, be sure that nothing will bring you down.

Week 45: Prevail

Reflect on how you begin your mornings. Whether it's powerful and productive or toxic and counterproductive. Today I challenge you to commit to improving in this area. Below, think about what you need to do first (upon opening your eyes) to be the best version of yourself. Some people commit to prayer, thanking God, or reading the Word. Others grab the phone, check notifications, and see how many people have liked their latest Instagram photos. There is a way that would help you establish a pattern of peace early in the a.m. Write your ideal morning below. What would happen the moment you open your eyes from when you begin your work for the day?

_____

_____

_____

_____

_____

_____

_____

_____

_____

You will never change your life until you change something you do daily. The secret to your success is found in your daily routine.

WEEK 46

Power Move:

Move in silence.

Week 46: Positioning

The older I get, the more I realize the value of privacy and cultivating my circle. Anywhere that success is blooming, there are enemies lurking. The enemy starts to attack because it's you, not always because of what you're building. The enemy knows you are a child of God and he knows your steps are God ordered, but if he knows God is about to shine the spotlight on you, he goes in to full attack mode.

Only speak about what you're doing when it's necessary to powerfully position you to receive what God has promised. When God is birthing your promise, be as silent as the letter "G" in lasagna, honey. Practice restraint and don't reveal… this is your silent season. You have to be able to handle the silence.

Moving in silence is simply hiding in plain sight if you will. They see you, but they don't see what's in you. Your blessing isn't everyone's business. Work hard during your silent season, and allow your success to make the noise for you.

Week 46: Prevail

One of the most important ways to prevail during and after your silent season is to remain confident without public affirmation. This is the season to build your character, self-confidence, and your trust in God's perfectly crafted purpose for you. Is God speaking to you in this season? If so, journal it here. Reflect on it, record it below, but don't reveal it.

_____

_____

_____

_____

_____

_____

_____

_____

_____

"*Don't announce the move before it's made. Everything you do doesn't need to be seen or heard.*"

– Natasha M. Brown

WEEK 47

Power Move:

Sow, support, share and soar.

Week 47: Positioning

Sow where you want to go. I learned to do this years ago when I had this vision of starting my own accessories boutique. I absolutely love accessories, but my goal was not only to sell earrings, necklaces, bracelets, and handbags, but I wanted to show women the appropriate way to wear accessories. Yes, there is such a thing! One day I was walking in the mall when I saw a familiar face. She was standing at her booth, and I stopped by to say hello. We realized we knew each other from church. I congratulated her and told her about the business I had planned to start. We exchanged information and started to keep in contact. One day, I received a check in the mail from her with a note stating that she wanted to sow into my business. Her act of kindness blessed me tremendously. I was able to purchase a few items to get my business started. When she started her next business, I was there to serve. Wiping tables, sweeping, mopping, taking her lunch, and doing whatever she needed me to do.

God did not bless us just for us. He blessed us to be a blessing. Thank God for the seed He placed in you, but make a conscious effort today to sow a seed into the life of someone else. You hold someone else's destiny inside of you. When you sow seeds of friendship, you get friends. When you sow seeds of support, you get more supporters. Even when you have nothing to give but prayers, your prayers will not return to you void.

Sowing and reaping has blessed me greatly, and I am thankful that the Lord has led me to share concerning this. I believe we, as women should do a better job at supporting other women. We tear each other down too often. Instead, we should be building each other up and encouraging one another to succeed. I encourage you to start sowing seeds in the area that you are believing God for, and know that before long, you will reap a harvest.

Sow into the lives of others. God does not just bless us so that we could be strong shade trees, but rather flourishing fruit trees. The concept of women helping other women benefits both parties, while demonstrating just how powerful a force women can be when we support one another.

Week 47: Prevail

Let's be intentional about this principle. Below, reflect on where you want to go, then, on what you need to sow. Lastly, identify fertile ground where you can sow seeds of resources, time, finances, prayer, encouragement... get creative! Remember, you will reap what you sow.

Where do you want to go?	What do you need to sow?	Who/what will you sow into?

Sow where you want to go!

POSITIONED TO PREVAIL

WEEK 48

Power Move:

Leverage the next level.

Week 48: Positioning

Leverage the next level. When we are confronted with new challenges, we must learn to handle them with grace. When you continue to say what you can't handle, you are really saying you don't want to go any higher. Every step is preparing you for new levels. There will always be new levels. New levels of motherhood, new levels of conflict, new levels of relationships, new levels of leadership... This is the very essence of what it means to prevail. It means leveling up, moving higher, advancing, and succeeding.

How you handled situations on level one will be totally different on level two. You are deserving of everything that life has to offer so don't let anyone limit your levels. Be careful because people change when you go to new levels which is so unfortunate. They stop cheering and start criticizing and will talk you out of your next level because they are not on your level.

God will cause you to experience certain situations so you can soar and be positioned for your next place of excellence. What you are experiencing now did not catch God by surprise at all, because He is preparing you by placing you in situations to promote you to the next level. There are lessons to learn on every level. If God is continuing to promote you to the next level that should tell you that God cares for you. My friend, level up for yourself and don't wait on anyone else to give you permission to do so.

Refuse to stay stuck, speak to your situation on every level, and tell whatever "that" is that's hindering you from moving to your next level, "This is not it for me, I'm on a new level!" Look around your home, your job, and at yourself in the mirror, and say out loud, "This is not it for me!" God built you to soar!

Week 48: Prevail

Think about the challenges you've faced this year. Can you discern an advancement to new levels on the horizon? Pray and ask God to reveal the purpose of the challenges you've faced this year. Journal what you hear, believe, or think afterwards.

_____

_____

_____

_____

_____

_____

_____

_____

_____

_____

Nevertheless, she persisted.

WEEK 49

Power Move:

Build your Board of Directors.

Week 49: Positioning

Your personal Board of Directors are trusted advisors who know and love you and will help you in your decision-making processes. Your Board of Directors voluntarily support you. They voluntarily tell you when you are on the right track and when something you are doing is positive, and on the flip side, they should tell you when you are off.

The Board of Directors is not a bunch of "yes men" (or women), nor do they feel inferior to you. You cannot have jealous people, 'frenemies', or those who want your position on your board of directors. This is your inner circle; your spiritual, professional, and life advisors. Your best interest is their best interest. Female friendships can multiply women's professional power, helping more women fulfill their potential and even helping to subsequently reduce the stigma that women can't get along. Yes, we can! Having each other's backs makes women unstoppable. When women work together, we succeed together. Surround yourself with people that are DOING something. You need relationships with people who share similar drive and visions in life, love, business, spirituality, and personal development.

There is so much tearing down of women in society when it should be our duty to uphold each other. We have the power to change the conversation when women are being torn down about their bodies, their choices, and how they choose to show up in the world. Instead, we can lead by example by having healthy, happy female friendships. Cheers to all of you who have the bomb board of directors. Notice that this week's power move is to "build" our Board of Directors. This means that as they are building you, you are building them. Care just as much about their well-being as they care about yours. Pray just as much for them (or more) as you ask them to pray for you. Make time for them as they make time for you.

Be intentional this week about building your board in every aspect of the word "build."

Week 49: Prevail

Who is on your Board of Directors? Who has appointed you to theirs? Is everyone in their proper positions? Are you playing your position(s) properly? Will your Board of Directors help you prevail? How?

Pen what's on your mind.

_____

_____

_____

_____

_____

_____

_____

_____

_____

"Behind every woman should be her Board of Directors cheering and clapping for her."

- Natasha M. Brown

WEEK 50

Power Move:

Never forget your name.

Week 50: Positioning

One of the most important possessions you will ever own is not your house, your intelligence, your good looks, nor your wealth. Your most valuable asset is your name. "A good name is more desirable than great riches; to be esteemed is better than silver or gold." - Proverbs 22:1. Your name is the greatest connection to your own identity and individuality. Some might say it is the most important word in the world to a person. We should pause to consider the value of a good name and the meaning because I can confidently say that most, if not all names, have meaning.

Many people love their names and get angry when someone mispronounces and misspells them, but how can you feel that way without even knowing what your name means? Your name is the main (and first) question people ask when they meet you. It is the most important means by which someone can identify and refer to you. Your name is your brand and the value others put on our names often dictates how we will be treated by them.

God is the greatest architect around and He was very meticulous when He designed you and the people He attached to you. He handcrafted your entire being down to the date and time you were born! We receive a name at birth and then spend our lives attaching meaning to it. We all know people who have built great value around their names. If you mention the name, people will remember something about that person's character.

Don't look to anyone to tell you who you are, because God already told you. Don't allow anyone to change your name! God has blessed your name and every blessing God bestows upon you is attached to your name. Your gift, your favor, your vision, your victory, and your next season are attached to YOU! You are fearfully and wonderfully made, and God made no mistake when He made you!

Week 50: Prevail

Use this time to write who you are.
Affirm who you are by identifying your "I am" statements. Below, write as many "I am" statements about yourself as you can come up with. Write who God says that you are. Repeat and remember these statements when your silent season gets lonely and challenging. (Bookmark this page, because it will indeed come in handy at some point.)

I am
I am
I am
I am
I am
I am
I am
I am
I am
I am
I am
I am
I am
I am
I am
I am
I am
I am

"Women like you don't happen by accident."

- Natasha M. Brown

WEEK 51

Power Move:

Leave a lasting legacy.

Week 51: Positioning

Legacy is defined as a gift by will; especially of money or other personal property a person leaves their heirs when he or she dies. However, there is a nonmaterial legacy I would like to challenge you to leave. This legacy comes from a lifetime of relationships, accomplishments, truths, and values, and it lives on in those whose lives we have touched. This type of legacy requires us as women to show up in the world every day and leave a footprint. This can only be accomplished by pushing ourselves to greatness and taking control of our destiny. Your story is your greatest history. Push yourself to greatness so your legacy can be left on the minds and in the hearts of others.

The world needs you, your gift, and your purpose, so leaving a legacy is living in the moment, making choices about the present, but keeping an awareness of the future. Your legacy is tied to what is important to you and what defines you as a person... your knowledge, community involvement, love, and passion. The decisions you make today will have a lasting effect when you are long gone, so be intentional about your legacy.

You have to be intentional with investing in others and you have to make time now. Schedule time in your week for those meaningful relationships that are most important to you and create lessons and experiences that will last forever. Our legacies are locked up inside of us and God has placed everything we need to flourish in us. It is up to us to pursue our passion which is attached to our legacy. We can't stop!

Imagine what legacies would have never existed if people had given up. Not to be deterred, they were resilient, kept going, and built successful lives. As a result, the people we know and remember best left sustainable legacies. There is always time to do more and achieve more; to help more and serve more; to teach more, and to learn more. Keep going and growing your legacy.

Week 51: Prevail

As we come to the end of a long journey together, I think it's a fine time to consider legacy. We write mission statements at the beginning of our careers or at the start of our businesses, and unfortunately, our "legacy statements" are written by others once we pass from earth in what is known as an obituary. No, I am not going to force you to write your obituary today, but I do want you to write a legacy statement. What will your legacy be? Write it in your words on your own terms, and then copy or pull this paper out and put it someplace where you can see it daily.

My Legacy Statement:

_____

_____

_____

_____

_____

_____

_____

_____

_____

"I would like to be known as an intelligent woman, a courageous woman, a loving woman, a woman who teaches by being."

— Dr. Maya Angelou

WEEK 52

Power Move:

Walk into your season!
You are **Positioned to Prevail.**

Week 52: Positioning

Congratulations and welcome to the new you! I expect great things from every woman reading this book. You are pretty powerful, phenomenal, resilient, confident, and *Positioned to Prevail*. We have walked through a year together. You've thought long and hard about where you are and where you've been. It's time to get to where you are going! Your direction has been determined by God, and your "new season" has been tailor made by God just for you.

Stop looking around, stop looking behind, look ahead! I messed around, looked back, missed two steps, fractured a bone in my foot, and sprained my ankle. I almost missed my blessing, but I laid on the garage floor in pain, praying for one of my daughters to find me, but in that moment, I told God "thank you!" Thank you for constantly reminding me to stop looking back.

God has placed us in a season where He wants us to be totally dependent upon Him. A place where our friends are unable to help us and we have no support system, because He wants us to experience Him in a new way. He has been waiting to get you by yourself so He can do a new thing in you, and in that place, you will come to know it has been God all the time. Not your degrees, your friends, your finances, your boo, but GOD! He has been behind the scenes orchestrating your seasons all along.

Refuse to stress about small, petty things, and don't panic. Whatever is happening in this season is what God has designed for you. Nothing catches God by surprise, my friend. Ask God for a new mind for your new journey. Being *Positioned to Prevail* is a state of mind, not just the title of this book. God will give you a new perspective and position you to look at things differently. There will be struggles along the way, but you will be able to show off those struggles in your new season. God has prepared and positioned you to prevail. God has trained you to hear His voice under pressure, and your steps are ordered. You are about to step into a new season of greatness, so stop right now and say, "God, I thank you!" Do not forget the lessons you have learned along the way, because those lessons are now a part of your testimony.

Walk in to any situation knowing the voice of God will guide you through! God wants your ear and mind. You have greatness inside of you, and it is time to release it. Whatever God promised, He will deliver. He will not forget His promises to you! Don't miss the voice of God in this season focusing on what was and what could have been. God is doing a new thing; receive it! God will give you everything you need for your next level that you never thought you needed or wanted. He will lay it before you and say, "I just want to see a smile on your face because you have been faithful and passed the test." Focus on God, and He will give you the unexpected!

Close the chapter on can't, chaotic, complicated, and confusion, and move to the next chapter of can, calm, confident, and clarity. You are resilient and *Positioned to Prevail.*

Week 52: Prevail

Finishing is a big deal, and you've completed this journey. Are you proud of yourself? You should be! You are the author of your life, so continue to write the chapters in your book. What were your best takeaways on this journey? Are you powerfully positioned to prevail?

_____

_____

_____

_____

_____

_____

_____

_____

_____

"Your crown has been bought and paid for. Put it on your head and wear it."

- Dr. Maya Angelou

About The Author

Natasha M. Brown is an author and resilience coach. Natasha equips and empowers women to soar personally and professionally. She has also served in the healthcare sector in Atlanta, Georgia for twenty years.

A native of Alabama, Natasha received her Bachelor's of Science Degree in Social Work from Alabama Agricultural and Mechanical University, Masters in Social Work from Clark Atlanta University, and Masters in Leadership and Organizational Development from Walden University.

Natasha is passionate about growing in grace, cultivating relationships with women, and avidly enjoys serving in the women's ministry at Elizabeth Baptist Church in Atlanta. Her hobbies include serving in the community and hosting events. Natasha has married her intellect with her ingenuity and strives to leave an impact on the hearts of women around the world.

Although Natasha has a great passion to serve women, her greatest joy and most important ministry is her family. She has two daughters, Kamryn and Karrington. Visit her online at NatashaMBrown.com

Did you enjoy *Positioned to Prevail?* Be sure to leave a review on Amazon.com and NatashaMBrown.com.
Share this book title with a woman you know!

CPSIA information can be obtained
at www.ICGtesting.com
Printed in the USA
LVHW081037070720
659969LV00019B/941